Artificial Insect-Inspired Vision for Autonomous Systems

Pavlo A. Molchanov
IPD Scientific LLC, USA

River Publishers

Routledge
Taylor & Francis Group
NEW YORK AND LONDON

Published 2025 by River Publishers
River Publishers
Alsbjergvej 10, 9260 Gistrup, Denmark
www.riverpublishers.com

Distributed exclusively by Routledge
605 Third Avenue, New York, NY 10017, USA
4 Park Square, Milton Park, Abingdon, Oxon OX14 4RN

Artificial Insect-Inspired Vision for Autonomous Systems / by Pavlo A. Molchanov.

Routledge is an imprint of the Taylor & Francis Group, an informa business

ISBN 978-87-7004-706-7 (hardback)
ISBN 978-87-7004-802-6 (paperback)
ISBN 978-87-7004-708-1 (online)
ISBN 978-87-7004-707-4 (master ebook)

Contents

Foreword

The application of human-like imaging vision in autonomous systems often necessitates the use of expensive, high-resolution optical systems. Processing the enormous amount of data required for high-resolution imaging and object recognition demands significant hardware and software resources, leading to what is known as the Big Data challenge. Human imaging vision, controlled by a large and complex brain, is comfortable for human needs but remains slower in reaction time compared to insects.

Insects like flies and mosquitoes have vision systems that rely on relatively simple directional sensors, which cover a 360-degree field of view. These sensors are controlled by much smaller brains because they don't need to calculate direction; the sensors are already oriented in the required directions. Instead of image recognition, insects use a simple fusion of sensory information for rapid threat detection.

The artificial insect-inspired vision system presented in this book mimics insect vision, making autonomous systems simpler, faster, and more efficient by addressing the Big Data challenge through the use of straightforward, high-speed threat detection techniques.

Human natural visual range is limited; sometimes, we want to see farther with better resolution and see through obstacles such as fog, snow, walls, or the ground. While radio frequency signals can penetrate these barriers more effectively, the resolution of the images captured is constrained by the diffraction limit imposed by classical physics. This book demonstrates how the proposed new generation of antenna arrays can provide limitless vision resolution and explores how these arrays can facilitate this task. By leveraging novel digital holographic technologies and the capabilities of monopulse multi-antenna arrays, we can push the boundaries of perception and expand our vision beyond the limitations of the human eye.

Artificial insect-inspired vision has the potential to assist people with impaired vision, offering solutions that could repair or even replace the human retina, the light-sensitive part of the eye. Wearable vision sensors can provide a comprehensive range of perceptual information, aiding navigation and communication for those with vision challenges.

Beyond medical applications, artificial vision systems can deliver human-like, controllable vision capabilities to technical and computer vision systems. This approach addresses challenges such as big data transfer and the limitations of precision optics, while also enhancing range, resolution, and field of view.

This book also introduces the technologies and techniques that enable enhanced vision, imaging, and perception, offering insights into the exciting world of Artificial Insect Vision with advanced antenna array systems. It aims to illustrate the possibility of the Artificial Eye and explores how advanced antenna arrays can enable this capability. By leveraging the unique properties and functionalities of antenna arrays, it becomes feasible to perceive and detect objects or phenomena that are typically hidden or imperceptible to the human senses. Through a comprehensive examination of the principles, design considerations, and applications of advanced antenna arrays, this book provides readers with a deeper understanding of how these arrays can enhance our ability to sense and perceive the unseen.

It will introduce you to various techniques and technologies employed in advanced antenna array systems, including control of resolution, field of view, focus, direction, and integration with other sensing modalities. Whether you are an engineer, researcher, student, or enthusiast interested in the fascinating realm of antenna arrays and their applications, this book will serve as a valuable resource to deepen your knowledge and appreciation of the remarkable possibilities that lie within the realm of "seeing the invisible."

Preface

"Artificial Insect-Inspired Vision for Autonomous Systems"

Dear reader, we are happy to present you the new book of our serial "Seeing Invisible." In the first book "Seeing Invisible. Advance Antenna Arrays" we provided a comprehensive and accessible explanation of nature-inspired Fly Eye antenna/sensor arrays, their advancements, and their limitations for a deeper understanding of their design, applications, and potential advancements inspired by nature.

This second book "Artificial Insect-Inspired Vision for Autonomous Systems" will help you understand advances inspired by Mother Nature insect vision technology for autonomous systems applications, including all kinds of drones, automotive systems, computer medical and biomedical automatic vision systems.

We will help you understanding new insect-inspired vision concept and technology for enhancing human vision. "Artificial Insect Vision" will allow seeing the world better than the human eye. Better, means smaller objects, longer distances, with better resolution, through high-scattering objects and materials in harsh environment conditions. New artificial insect vision technology will be basic for autonomous systems because more fast, more accurate, simple, and same time can provide revolutionary human-like vision with electronic lensless control of resolution, field of view, focus, and direction, which will help to solve big data problems of transferring vision information.

Also, we will present a new concept of Artificial eye. Eye, which can be used by blind humans and can be used as a wearable portable like glasses devices and will not require any surgery or implants, but same time will provide more advances in vision on long distances with high-resolution and artificial automatic recognition of around objects.

While the book is accessible to a wide range of readers and does not require specialized education, it will serve as a valuable resource for engineers and technicians involved in the design and development of all-space communication and navigation systems, drones, and hypersonic missile detection systems, and medical imaging devices. The book particularly emphasizes interference immunity and protection in these applications. Furthermore, it can be employed as a textbook for advanced radar technology courses and seminars, providing a comprehensive understanding of the subject matter.

List of Figures

List of Abbreviations

ADS-B	Automatic dependent surveillance-broadcast
AESA	Active electronically scanned array
AGC	Automatic gain control
AI	Artificial intelligence
AIA	Automated Imaging Association
AOA	Angle of arrival
CCD	Charge-coupled device
CDI	Coherent diffraction imaging
CW	Continuous wave
CZT	Cittert–Zernike theorem
DOA	Direction of arrival
DOF	Depth of field
EM	Electromagnetic
EMP	Electromagnetic pulse
EW	Electromagnetic wave
FCDI	Fresnel coherent diffraction imaging
FOV	Field of view
fps	Frames per second
FTH	Fourier transform holography
GSD	Ground sample distance
HOB	Holographic database
MSP	Monopulse signal processor
OAML	Orbital angular momentum lattice
ppi	Pixels per inch
RAM	Receiver antenna module
RF	Radio frequency
RPA	Robotic automation platform
SAA	Small sense and avoid
SDR	Software-defined radio
TAM	Transceiver antenna module
UAS	Unmanned aerial systems
USB	Universal serial bus

1

New Generation of Antenna Arrays: Brief

Introduction

Fly Eye antenna arrays have revolutionized the landscape of surveillance and detection by enabling the simultaneous coverage of the entire sky without any moving parts. These arrays offer rapid and precise direction-finding capabilities for multiple threats or objects. Utilizing contemporary digital monopulse multi-channel processing and simultaneous digital synchronization, Fly Eye arrays facilitate nearly instant multi-target detection, more accurate tracking, and improved protection [1–14].

Drawing inspiration from centuries of natural evolution, the nature-inspired sensor array concept has led to the development of a new technology for detecting and recognizing concealed objects. This technology, detailed in this book, leverages direct digital coherent processing of scattered and diffracted frequency components alongside spatial spectral pattern analysis. This approach enables remote non-invasive detection and recognition of objects or anomalies in high-scattering mediums based on their spectrum signatures.

1.1 Nature-inspired Multi-sensor Fly Eye Antenna Array

The Fly Eye antenna array, inspired by nature, employs multiple angularly tilted sensors with individual connections to memory, enabling simultaneous coverage of the entire sky. In real life, two fly eyes can cover the entire sky, eliminating the need for wide-angle scanning. They can send signals about threat positions practically instantaneously, without requiring extensive processing, as the position of each sensor inherently provides directional information (Figure 1.1).

The nature-inspired multi-antenna Fly Eye array is arranged as a spatially angularly tilted directional sensor/antenna array. Each directional antenna

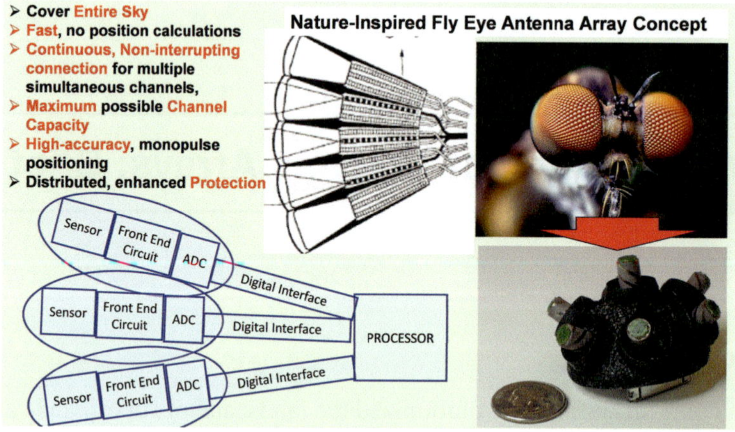

Figure 1.1 Fly eye-inspired antenna array mimics its structure. Separate sensors with direct detection and digitizing on antennas and digital lossless transferring to the processor.

is coupled with a separate processing channel, which includes a direct detector and digitizer. This setup allows for the instant and simultaneous non-interrupting capture of amplitude, phase, and angular/spatial information from multiple targets/channels. A digital interface transfers the received data to the processor at high speed via multiple channels, ensuring no amplitude or phase losses and synchronization all received data relative to the processor time for all sensors/channels.

The use of monopulse high directional accuracy methods for processing signals from overlapping multi-axis positioned directional antennas facilitates fast and simultaneous signal processing. Additionally, the direct detection and digitization of received signals on antennas simplify the design, enabling all-sky monitoring with rapid, non-scanning target tracking.

The solid-state design of multi-antenna modules, combined with their distribution and digital interfaces, enhances the integrity and functionality of radar and communication systems. Simultaneously, this approach provides improved protection against electromagnetic pulse (EMP) and interference through the application of directional shielded antennas and the strategic distribution of antennas around the vehicle perimeter.

1.2 Advances of Staring, Non-scanning Antenna Array

Traditional phased arrays scan the coverage volume and have limited connection time on any given signal source, which results in the inability

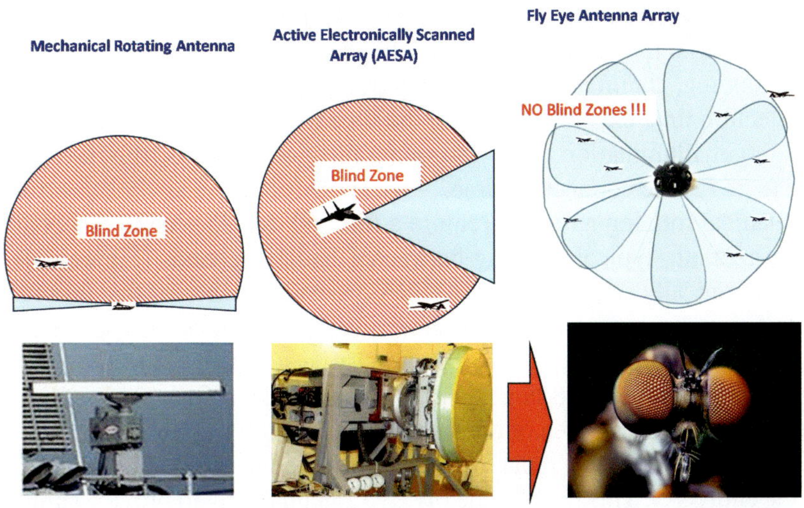

Figure 1.2 Mechanical rotating antenna providing narrow plate-like coverage and huge blind zone in the upper part. AESA arrays have a better front-view cone area of observation but require approx. 0.5–1 second scanning time.

to provide simultaneous instant coverage of entire sky signal sources. This limitation can be overcome by employing staring antenna systems. Continuous staring can be achieved with a nature-inspired multi-antenna array architecture that incorporates multiple staring directional antennas, enabling virtual scanning and real-time recording of digital holograms (Figure 1.2).

This approach allows the system to maintain continuous observation of the entire field of view, providing comprehensive and uninterrupted coverage. The integration of multiple staring antennas facilitates the simultaneous detection and tracking of multiple targets, capturing high-resolution data without the need for mechanical scanning. This capability is crucial for applications requiring persistent surveillance and real-time response.

The angle of arrival (AOA) for active electronically scanned arrays (AESAs) is limited in both azimuth and elevation, resulting in incomplete sky coverage and the presence of gaps or blind zones. In contrast, a Fly Eye antenna array can provide comprehensive coverage of the entire sky or a full sphere without any blind zones (Figure 1.3). This type of antenna array consists of multiple angularly tilted antennas or sensors, mimicking the structure of a fly's eye. The Fly Eye antenna array enables practically instantaneous communication or information about multiple targets or signal sources, ensuring seamless and continuous coverage.

The target detection time for threats is crucial for the survival of a fly, and the fly eye architecture provides practically instant threat detection and direction finding, facilitated by the monopulse method. In radar systems, target detection time encompasses both the time to scan the observation area and the target illumination time. In communication systems, this is often referred to as “active connection time.”

Mechanical rotating antennas require a full 360-degree scan to detect all targets in azimuth, typically taking between 1 and 10 seconds (Figure 1.4). Active electronically scanned arrays (AESAs) use narrow beams that provide better directional accuracy for target detection. A smaller beam spot yields better directionality, but the narrow beam must be scanned across the entire observation area to detect all targets, it takes more time, usually taking about 0.5–1 second to cover an area of approximately 120×60 degrees.

In contrast, a Fly Eye radar uses a multi-antenna array that instantly covers the entire sky. This enables the Fly Eye antenna array to provide simultaneous and continuous information about all targets without interruption. The detection time for the Fly Eye radar is composed of the detection time, which is approximately a few microseconds for a semiconductor detector, and the time for direction finding through signal processing. This architecture allows for near-instantaneous threat detection and continuous monitoring, significantly improving response times compared to traditional scanning methods.

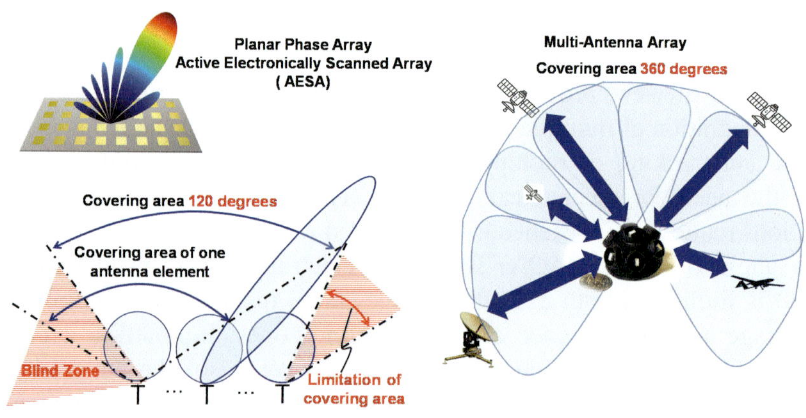

Figure 1.3 The cover area of one scanning beam planar phase array is limited by 120 degrees by elevation. It is smaller than each omnidirectional antenna element because of phase shift limitation. Fly Eye antenna arrays have no blind zones and provide an uninterruptable connection with multiple signal sources.

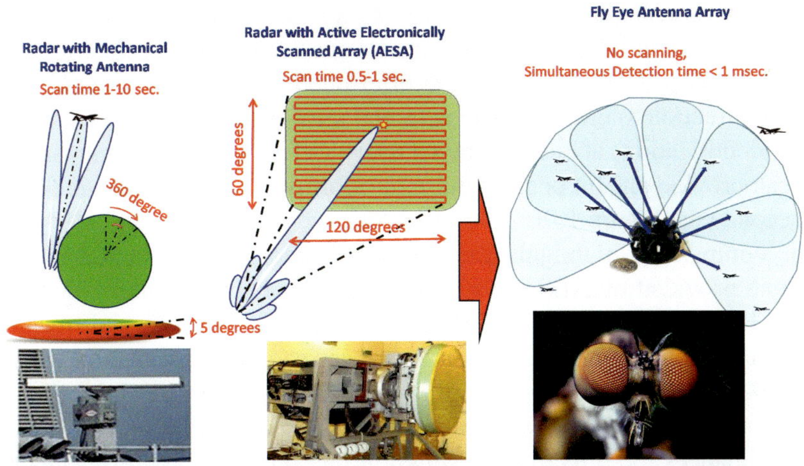

Figure 1.4 Comparing target detection time for scanning and non-scanning antenna arrays. Non-scanning antenna array provides instant detection of multiple targets and continuous non-interruptible tracking of every target. For communication non-scanning system it means non-interruptible communication with multiple customers, which leads to a hundred times higher speed of communication compared to systems with switching beams.

1.3 Active Connection Time. Transmission Rate. Link Capacity

The target illumination time for radar systems is a critical parameter, as it provides more accurate radar range, target position information, and essential data for target recognition and identification. In telecommunications, this parameter translates to the connection's line transmission rate or the time required for a non-interrupted connection. According to Wikipedia: "In telecommunications, effective transmission rate (average rate of transmission, effective speed of transmission) is the rate at which information is processed by a transmission facility."

- The effective transmission rate is calculated as (a) the measured number of units of data, such as bits, characters, blocks, or frames, transmitted during a significant measurement time interval divided by (b) the measurement time interval.
- The effective transmission rate is usually expressed as a number of units of data per unit time, such as bits per second or characters per second.

Channel capacity represents the theoretical maximum rate at which information can be reliably transmitted over a communication channel.

For radar systems, one complete scan of a mechanical rotating antenna provides a single hit (short pulse reflected from the target) for each target. This means that a rotating antenna can offer one brief pulse of information (including direction to the target and potential information for target recognition and identification) about each target every 1–10 seconds. In contrast, an AESA can provide one hit or short pulse of information for each target every 0.5–1 second (see Figure 1.5).

This comparison highlights the significant improvement in the target update rate provided by AESA systems over traditional mechanical rotating antennas. However, the proposed Fly Eye radar system, with its multi-beam antenna array, would offer an even more advanced capability by enabling continuous and simultaneous coverage, thus providing real-time, uninterrupted information about all targets without the need for scanning. This architecture not only enhances the effective transmission rate but also maximizes channel capacity by ensuring that data is continuously and reliably transmitted. This represents a significant advancement over both traditional mechanical and AESA radar systems in terms of both speed and reliability of target information acquisition.

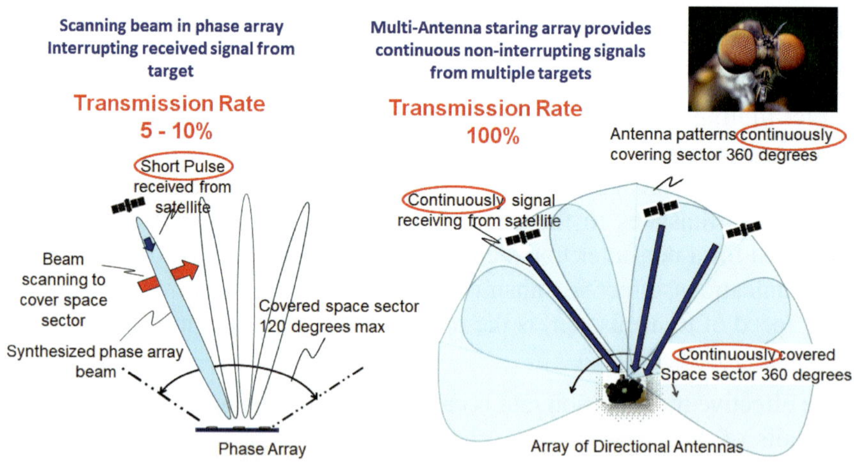

Figure 1.5 Phase array with scanning, switching, or both scanning and switching beam is active connecting with one signal source (target or satellite for communication system) short time, 5%–10% of all scanning time. Speed of transferring information, or transmission rate small. A staring antenna array provides a non-interrupting active connection with multiple signal sources, it means can provide 10 times higher speed or channel capacity.

1.4 Directional Accuracy

In optical systems, the diffraction-limited angular resolution is determined by the wavelength of the light and the diameter of the objective's entrance aperture. This diffraction limit sets a fundamental constraint on the angular resolution of the system [4].

Similarly, in radar systems, the minimal beamwidth is constrained by the wavelength of the radar signal (Figure 1.6). Higher frequency radar signals, such as those in the millimeter-wave range, enable smaller beamwidths and increased beam gain. However, as the frequency increases and the beamwidth becomes smaller, the scanning time proportionally increases with the size of the observation area.

To enhance directional accuracy, monopulse techniques are frequently employed. The overlapping of antenna patterns allows for a more precise measurement of the direction of arrival by calculating the ratio of amplitudes or phases from different elements. One significant advantage of the monopulse method is that it does not require a specific baseline distance between antennas.

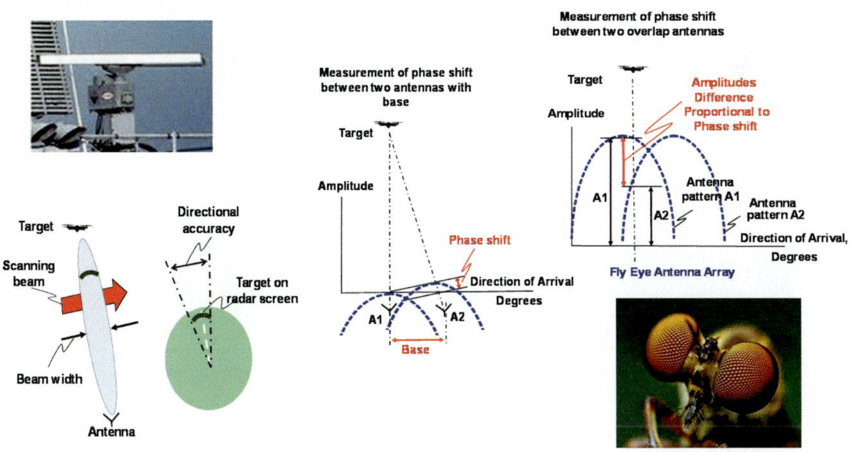

Figure 1.6 Measurement of the range to target by measurement of phase shift. Regular systems are using scanning beam or two antennas positioned at some distance, base. Longer base, better accuracy. Monopulse systems are providing much better accuracy by using two antennas with overlap antenna patterns. The ratio of amplitudes is proportional to phase shift and range to target. Same time one of the antennas can be used for suppression of interference signals and noises.

1.5 Enhanced Jam-spoof Protection

Digital interface with processor provides reliable transfer of received signals to processor and synchronization of all receiving signals with reference to transmitting signals and processor time for creating a real-time holographic matrix. It allows the distribution of directional shielded antennas around the perimeter for additional protection against jamming signals by the carrier body. The advantage of this configuration is that it enables non-interrupting communication with all satellites within the coverage area and same time enhances EMP protection (Figure 1.7).

Designers of antenna arrays need to remember, that deflection of scanning beams in phased array is not similar to the deflection of light by the lens (Figure 1.8). Each omnidirectional (isotropic) antenna element transmits/receives microwave energy omnidirectionally. A small part of energy sum in one or

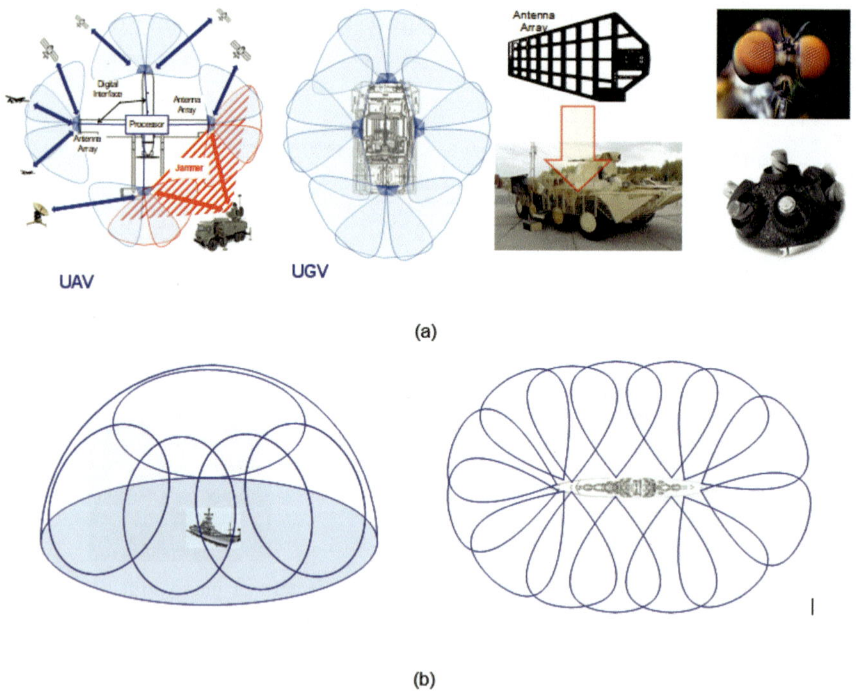

Figure 1.7 Distributed antenna directional (shielded) antenna arrays can enhance EMP protection of airborne, ground (a), and sea (b) carriers.

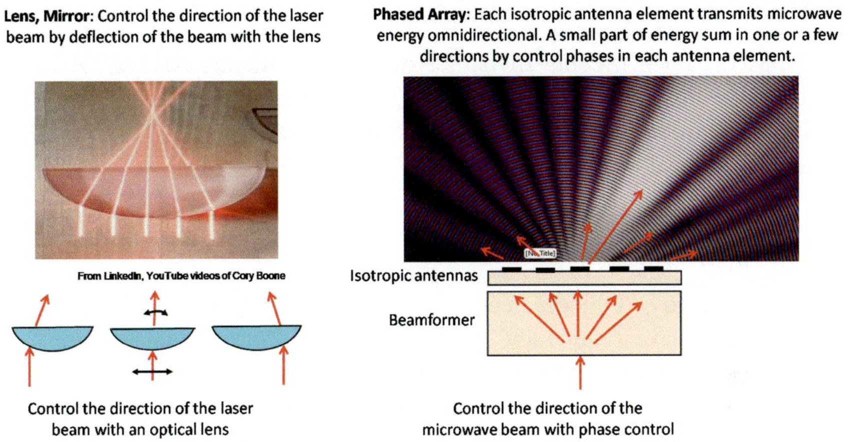

Figure 1.8 Explanation of beamforming by phased antenna array compare to light beam deflection/focusing by lens.

a few directions by control of phases in each antenna element by the beamformer. The rest of the energy is still transmitting/receiving omnidirectionally by antenna elements, and this energy (side lobes) is powerful enough and may be a threat to human health.

Conclusion

Fly Eye antenna array provides the following advances:

- The antenna array can simultaneously cover the entire sky.
- Fast, practically instant detection and calculation of multiple target positions by simple one-step algorithms.
- Continuous, non-interrupting connection for multiple simultaneous channels.
- Providing the maximum possible 100% transmission rate and channel capacity.
- High-accuracy, monopulse positioning.
- Enhanced jam protection by distribution of directional shielded antennas.

The use of monopulse techniques, combined with the advancements in radar frequencies and beamwidth management, underscores the capability to achieve high directional accuracy and rapid target detection, even in complex and dynamic observation environments.

References

[1] P. A. Molchanov "Seeing Invisible: Advanced Antenna Arrays," River Publishers, Publication date: 04/12/2024, [Online] Available https://www.barnesandnoble.com/w/seeing-invisible-pavlo-a-molchanov/1144371618, [Accessed April, 15, 2024].

[2] A. Gorwara, P. Molchanov "Fly Eye Radar Concept," The 18th International Radar Symposium IRS 2017, Prague, Czech Republic, June 28-30, 2017.

[3] P. A. Molchanov, "Objects Recognition in High-scattering Conditions at Radio/Microwave Frequency," SPIE Defense + Commercial Sensing", Conference, National Harbor, Washington DC, April, 2024.

[4] P. A. Molchanov, "Multi-Antenna Array for All Space Communications," 2024 IEEE Radio Wireless Week (RWW), Conference, January, 2024.

[5] A. Gorwara, P. Molchanov, "Distributed micro-radar system for detection and tracking of low profile, low-altitude targets," Proc. of 2016 SPIE Security+Defense conference, Baltimore, MD, USA, Paper #9825-7, April 2016.

[6] P. Molchanov O. Asmolova, "Fly Eye radar or micro-radar sensor technology," Proc. of SPIE 2014, Defense+Security, Session C31, Sensors, Control, Communications, Technologies for Homeland Security and Homeland Defense XIII, Baltimore, MD, USA, Vol.9074 907405, May 6, 2014, [Online], Available http://spie.org/Publications/Proceedings/Paper/10.1117/12.2050063, [Accessed_April 20, 2024].

[7] A. Gorwara, P. Molchanov, O. Asmolova, "Doppler micro sense and avoid radar," SPIE Security+Defense 2015, Toulouse, France, 21-24 September 2015.

[8] P. Molchanov, O. Asmolova, "Sense and Avoid Radar for Micro-Nano Robots," (Invited Paper), SPIE Security+Defense Conference, Amsterdam, September 24, 2014, [Online] Available http://spie.org/Publications/Proceedings/Paper/10.1117/12.2071366, [Accessed April 20, 2024].

[9] P. Molchanov, "All Digital Radar Architecture," Paper 9248-11, SPIE Security+Defense Conference, Amsterdam, September 25, 2014, [Online] Available http://spie.org/Publications/Proceedings/Paper/10.1117/12.2060249 [Accessed January 10, 2023].

[10] P. Molchanov, V. Contarino, "Directional antenna array for communications, control and data link protection," SPIE 2013 Defense +Security Conference, Session 9, Communication, Control, and Enabling

Technologies, Paper 8711-31, April 30, 2013, [Online], Available http://spie.org/Publications/Proceedings/Paper/10.1117/12.2015607, [Accessed January 10, 2023].

[11] V. Contarino, P. Molchanov, R. Healing, O. Asmolova, "UAV Radar System of Low observable Targets," Conf. Unmanned Systems, Canada. Nova Scotia, Canada, K1P1B1, Nov. 7-10, 2011.

[12] P. Molchanov, V. Contarino, "New Distributed Radar Technology based on UAV or UGV Application," Defense +Security. Session 6, MIMO Radar, Paper 8714-27, April 30, 2013.

[13] P. Molchanov, V. Contarino, "Multi-beam Antenna Array for Protecting GPS Receivers from Jamming and Spoofing Signals," U.S. Patent and Trademark Office (USPTO) application, Receipt 13562313 dated 31 July 20, 2012, [Online] Available http://www.google.com/patents/US20140035783, [Accessed January, 10, 2024].

[14] Jon Bentley and Jerome Patoux, "The Continuing Evolution of Radar, From Rotating Dish to Digital Beamforming," Microwave Journal, [e-Book], Available Safari e-book, p.5-8, [Accessed January,10, 2023].

2

Limitless Scalable Resolution with EM Waves

Introduction

The novel nature-inspired vision technology presents a groundbreaking solution to the problem of scalable vision resolution. This new vision technology surpasses the human eye's capabilities by allowing it to see smaller objects at longer distances with superior resolution. It is effective even through high-scattering objects and materials, and in harsh environmental conditions.

The limitless scalable vision resolution and its revolutionary human-like capabilities offer electronic lensless control of resolution, field of view, focus, and direction. This innovation addresses significant challenges in transferring visual information to computer vision systems, thereby enhancing their performance and accuracy.

Key advantages of lensless scalable vision technology:

- Enhanced resolution: Capable of detecting smaller objects at greater distances with unparalleled clarity.
- Effective in harsh environments: Maintains high resolution through high-scattering objects and materials.
- Electronic lensless control: Provides dynamic control over resolution, field of view, focus, and direction without the need for precision optics and mechanical adjustments.
- Big data solutions: Facilitates efficient transfer and processing of visual information, addressing the big data challenges in computer vision systems.

This advanced vision technology promises to revolutionize various fields, including surveillance, medical imaging, remote sensing, and more, by providing superior imaging capabilities that go beyond the limits of traditional optical systems.

2.1 Imaging Resolution vs. Vision Resolution

Imaging resolution is a multifaceted concept that varies depending on the application and the type of system used. Wikipedia provides several definitions of resolution, encompassing optical, digital, spectral, remote sensing, and camera resolutions, among others. The key types of resolution are relevant to different applications. Optical resolution describes the ability of an imaging system to resolve detail in the object being imaged. Digital capture resolution refers to the ability of an imaging device to capture finely spaced details optically.

To better understand and categorize resolution, we can divide it into two main parts:

Vision resolution refers to the smallest detail that an electromagnetic wave (EW) receiving/sensing system can resolve. It measures the system's ability to distinguish between two closely spaced points or smallest objects. This type of resolution is crucial for remote detection systems based on the application of electromagnetic waves (EW).

Imaging resolution pertains to the level of detail that an image holds when displayed. It is influenced by the type of image display, whether spatial or digital and the physical properties of the display material and imaging means. Imaging resolution is defined by how finely the image details are captured and displayed.

2.1.1 Imaging resolution

Imaging resolution indicates the level of detail in an image [1]. Higher resolution means more detailed images. It can be quantified by how closely lines can be placed together and still be visibly resolved. Units include lines per millimeter (lines/mm), lines per inch (lines/inch), lines per picture height (TV lines or TVL), or angular subtense. Imaging resolution is often measured in line pairs, which consist of one dark line and one adjacent light line. For example, a resolution of 10 lines per millimeter translates to 5 dark lines and 5 light lines, or 5 line pairs per millimeter (5 LP/mm). Photographic lenses are most often quoted in line pairs per millimeter.

Spatial resolution usually characterized by the terms blurriness and sharpness are used for digital images but other descriptors are used to reference the hardware capturing and displaying the images [2].

Spatial resolution in radiology is the ability of the imaging modality to differentiate two objects. Low spatial resolution techniques will be unable to differentiate between two objects that are relatively close together (Figures 2.1 and 2.2).

High resolution is critical in various fields for accurate detection and representation of objects. In medical imaging, high spatial resolution enables better differentiation of anatomical structures.

In remote sensing, it allows for a more detailed analysis of geographical features. For digital displays and cameras, higher resolution translates to sharper and more detailed images, enhancing the viewer's experience and the accuracy of information conveyed. The different types of resolution and their measurements help in choosing the right imaging system for specific applications, ensuring that the images produced meet the required level of detail and accuracy.

Imaging resolution usually shows how closely lines can be resolved in an image, which is called spatial resolution, and it depends on the properties of the system creating the image, not just the pixel resolution in pixels per inch (ppi). For practical purposes, the clarity of the image is decided by its spatial resolution, not the number of pixels in an image. In effect, spatial

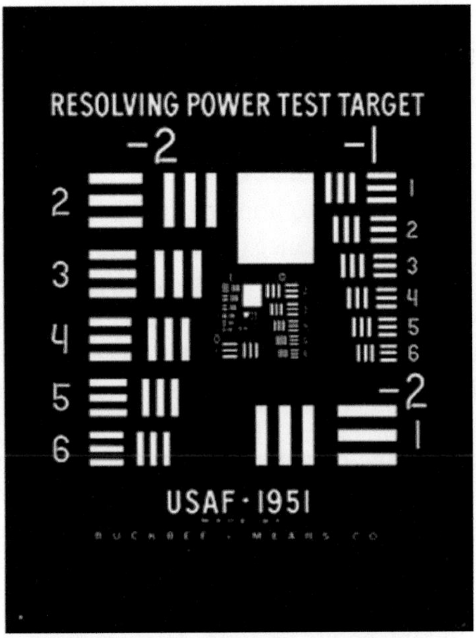

Figure 2.1 The 1951 USAF resolution test target is a classic test target used to determine the spatial resolution of imaging sensors and imaging systems.

Figure 2.2 The image at left has a higher *pixel count* than the one to the right, but is still of worse spatial resolution [1].

resolution is the number of independent pixel values per unit length. The spatial resolution of consumer displays ranges from 50 to 800 pixel lines per inch. With scanners, optical resolution is sometimes used to distinguish spatial resolution from the number of pixels per inch. In remote sensing, spatial resolution is typically limited by diffraction, as well as by aberrations, imperfect focus, and atmospheric distortion.

2.1.2 Vision resolution

Vision resolution is usually related to transmitting/receiving EM signals system application. Ground sample distance (GSD) refers to the pixel spacing on the Earth's surface in remote sensing imagery. It's typically smaller than the resolvable spot size, ensuring high-resolution images. In astronomy spatial resolution is often quantified in data points per arcsecond, considering the varying distances of objects observed. This measure accounts for the apparent size of objects based on their distance from Earth.

In electron microscopy, line resolution refers to the minimum separation between adjacent parallel lines, while point resolution is the minimum separation between adjacent points. Both are crucial for detecting fine details and atomic interactions.

High-speed cameras measure time resolution in frames per second (fps), capturing events at different points in time. Higher fps values enable the visualization of rapid events with finer temporal detail.

Radiometric resolution determines how finely a system can represent or distinguish differences in intensity. It's often expressed as the number of levels or bits, indicating the system's ability to capture subtle intensity variations.

Digital imaging resolution is commonly associated with pixel count. International standards define resolution as the total number of pixels in an image, typically measured in megapixels. The number of effective pixels refers to the pixel sensors contributing to the final image, excluding unused or light-shielded pixels.

2.2 Optical Resolution Limits

Optical resolution is a critical factor in determining the clarity and detail of images produced by optical instruments such as microscopes, telescopes, and cameras. The optical resolution limit is the minimum distance between two objects that can be distinguished by an optical instrument or system [1, 2]. It is determined by the wavelength of the radiation used to view the objects and the size and number of pixels on the sensor. For visible light, the resolution limit is about half the wavelength. The general rule is that the limit of resolution is about one-half the wavelength of the EM waves used to view the specimen. This means anything smaller than half the wavelength won't be resolved.

In optics, any optical instrument or system – a microscope, telescope, or camera – has a principal limit to its resolution due to the physics of diffraction. An optical instrument is said to be diffraction-limited if it has reached this limit of resolution performance. Other factors may affect an optical system's performance, such as lens imperfections or aberrations, but these are caused by errors in the manufacture or calculation of a lens, whereas the diffraction limit is the maximum resolution possible for a theoretically perfect, or ideal, optical system [2–10, 11–15].

The diffraction-limited angular resolution, in radians, of an instrument is proportional to the wavelength of the light being observed and inversely proportional to the diameter of its objective's entrance aperture. For telescopes with circular apertures, the size of the smallest feature in an image that is diffraction limited is the size of the Airy disk. As one decreases the size of the aperture of a telescopic lens, diffraction proportionately increases. At small apertures, such as f/22, most modern lenses are limited only by diffraction and not by aberrations or other imperfections in the construction.

For microscopic instruments, the diffraction-limited spatial resolution is proportional to the light wavelength, and to the numerical aperture of either the objective or the object illumination source, whichever is smaller.

In astronomy, a diffraction-limited observation achieves the resolution of a theoretically ideal objective in the size of the instrument used. However, most observations from Earth are limited due to atmospheric effects. Optical telescopes on the Earth work at a much lower resolution than the diffraction limit because of the distortion introduced by the passage of light through several kilometers of turbulent atmosphere. Advanced observatories have started using adaptive optics technology, resulting in greater image resolution for faint targets, but it is still difficult to reach the diffraction limit using adaptive optics [19–24].

2.3 High-resolution Coherent Diffraction Imaging with RF CW Signals

Continuous wave (CW) radio frequency (RF) signals possess unique capabilities for high-resolution imaging despite challenges posed by the diffraction phenomenon. These signals offer significant advantages, including penetration through diverse materials with minimal ionizing damage, making them valuable across various domains. The advantage of RF CW signals is penetration through various materials. RF signals penetrate materials such as walls, ground, and human tissues effectively, enabling imaging through obstacles. Second, low risk of Ionizing damage. Unlike optical irradiation or X-rays, low-power RF signals pose minimal risk of ionizing damage to humans, ensuring safety in applications involving human exposure.

The challenge of RF imaging systems like optical systems is the diffraction limitation of resolution. The diffraction phenomenon limits the vision/imaging resolution of RF signals. Now we will use the term imaging resolution, as it is applied in coherent diffraction imaging (CDI) theory, but it means that imaging resolution in coherent diffraction imaging systems is determined by vision resolution, and we will not consider display imaging resolution resources.

As the wavelength of RF signals can range from centimeters to meters, achieving high-resolution imaging becomes challenging. To address the challenge of limited imaging resolution, an innovative approach called high-resolution coherent diffraction imaging (CDI) with RF CW signals has been developed. This technique leverages the coherence properties of RF signals to achieve high-resolution imaging.

2.3.1 Key features of high-resolution CDI with RF CW signals

Utilization of coherence properties, like high-resolution CDI with RF CW signals exploits the coherence properties of RF waves to overcome diffraction limitations. Digital processing techniques including advanced digital processing techniques are employed to analyze the coherent diffraction patterns of RF signals, allowing for the reconstruction of high-resolution images. High-resolution coherent diffraction imaging with RF CW signals offers a promising solution to the challenge of limited imaging resolution in RF imaging applications. By harnessing the coherence properties of RF signals and employing advanced digital processing techniques, this approach enables the visualization of fine details with unprecedented clarity, opening up new possibilities for high-resolution imaging across diverse domains.

Diagram presenting traditional RF CW imaging system for receiving scattered, reflected, and diffracted beams with charge-coupled device (CCD) imaging detector for object size larger than RF wavelength is presented in Figure 2.3 [5–8].

A CCD is an integrated circuit containing an array of linked, or coupled, capacitors. Under the control of an external circuit, each capacitor can transfer

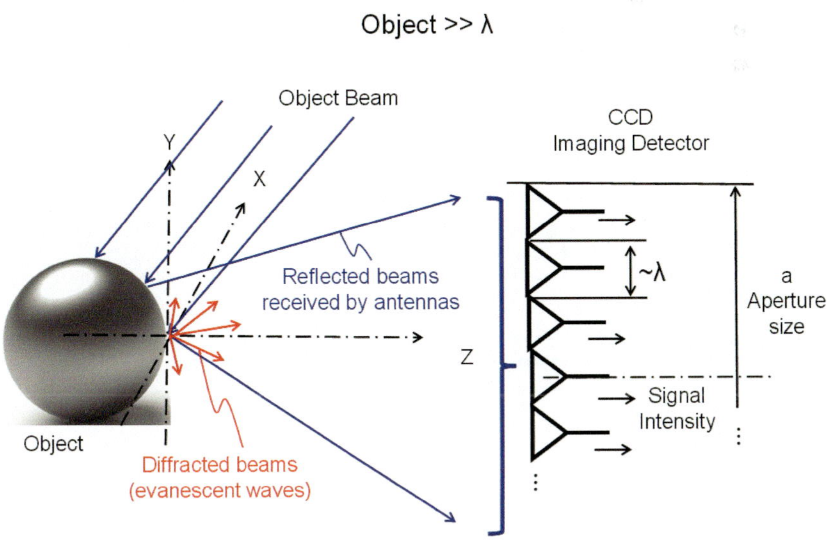

Figure 2.3 Short wavelength (smaller than object size) beams illuminating object surface. Diffracted beams (evanescent waves) decay at a very short (a few wavelengths) distance. Reflected beams are receiving by CCD imaging detector consisting array of beam intensity sensors.

its electric charge to a neighboring capacitor. CCD sensors are a major technology used in digital imaging [Wikipedia].

Diagram demonstrating recording of diffracted/scattered by object components in Fresnel near-field area by narrow beam transmitting/receiving antenna scanning along X, Y axis is presented in Figure 2.4.

The process of recording diffracted/scattered components within the Fresnel near-field area is based on using narrow beam transmitting/receiving sensors. The procedure involves two steps. Transmitting sensor with narrow beams cover a small section of the object during the transmission phase. A narrow-beam sensor receives only a limited portion of the diffracted/scattered components, constrained by the sensor's covered angle of view.

When short-wavelength beams illuminate an object's surface, registering scattered and reflected beams becomes feasible with a narrow-beam scanning transmitting/receiving sensor. However, a significant portion of reflected and scattered beams may not be captured by the sensor, as indicated by the red areas in Figure 2.5.

Components that could potentially be diffracted or scattered by the parts of the object not covered by the narrow beam are not received. Sensor scanning along the X and Y axes or the surface of the object does not capture the full angular spectrum of diffracted or scattered components, as it fails to cover the maximum scattering angle.

As the sensor scans along these axes or the object's surface, it only captures a narrow part of the components reflected by the part of the object's

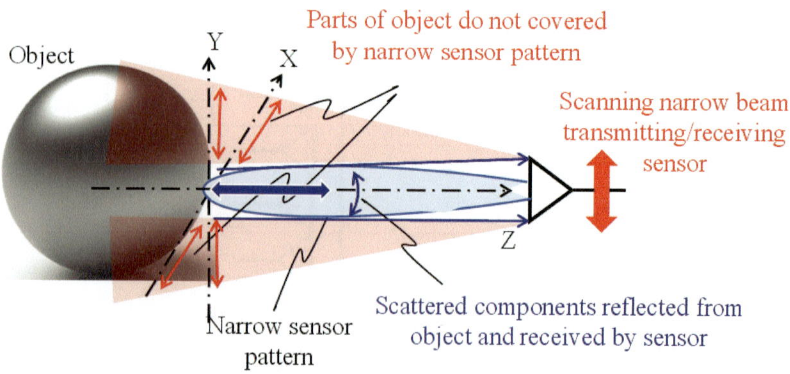

Figure 2.4 Short wavelength (smaller than object size) beams illuminating object surface. Registration of scattered and reflected beams provided by scanning objects by narrow beam transmitting/receiving sensor. The reflected beams and part of scattered beams are received by the sensor. Part of the scattered beams are not received by sensor (red areas in the picture).

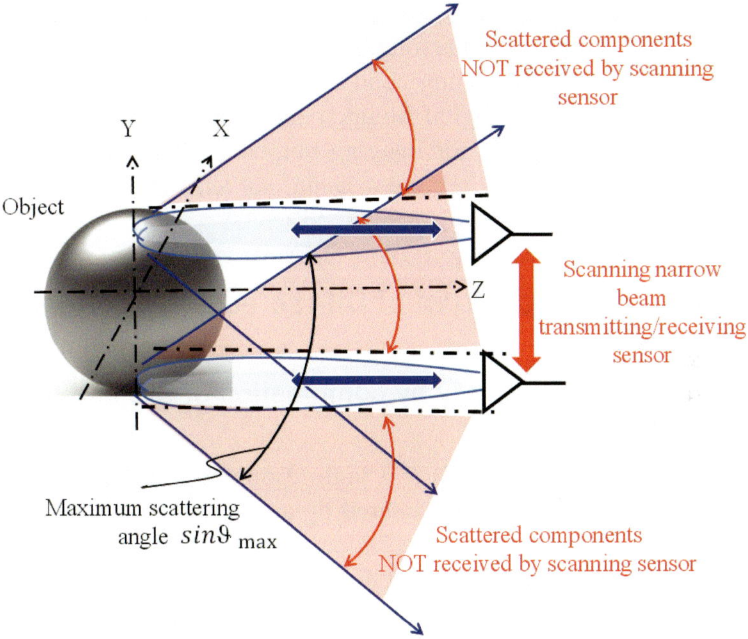

Figure 2.5 Short wavelength (smaller than object size) beams illuminating object surface. Registration of scattered and reflected beams provided by scanning objects by narrow beam transmitting/receiving sensor. A significant part of reflected and scattered beams are not received by the narrow beam transmitting/receiving sensor (red areas in the picture).

surface covered by the sensor pattern, in the opposite direction. Consequently, this limitation results in the incomplete reception of the spectrum signature necessary for object recognition, ultimately diminishing image resolution.

The integration of CDI and Fourier transform holography (FTH) into a new concept of digital holographic imaging offers a solution to the diffraction limitations faced by RF signals. This technique not only addresses the phase ambiguity problem but also significantly enhances imaging resolution.

Digital holographic imaging combines the principles of CDI and FTH, leveraging their respective strengths to overcome the limitations of traditional RF imaging. By doing so, it provides a practical solution for achieving theoretically limitless imaging resolution in RF systems.

One of the key advantages of digital holographic imaging is its practical invariance to the frequency of applying RF signals. Instead, its effectiveness is primarily determined by the digitizing sampling frequency and frequency stability, which are inherent properties of the processing resources available.

This approach opens up new possibilities for diverse applications in various fields, as it enables high-resolution imaging even in environments with high scattering and challenging conditions. By integrating contemporary radar technologies with digital holographic imaging, we can unlock the full potential of RF signals for imaging purposes, paving the way for advancements in fields such as remote sensing, surveillance, and medical imaging.

2.4 Digital Angular Spectrum of Diffracted and Scattered Components

2.4.1 Solving phase ambiguity by combination of CDI and digital FTH techniques

Coherent diffraction imaging (CDI) is a high-resolution imaging approach where the waves diffracted and/or scattered by an object carry information about its properties like size, shape, absorption, and dielectric characteristics. These waves are captured as a diffraction pattern and used for reconstructing an image. CDI can achieve high-resolution information by capturing high-order diffraction components. This technique can even maintain its effectiveness when the wavelength is significantly larger than the object's dimensions, ensuring spatial invariance. Coherent diffracting imaging techniques involve the superimposition of waves scattered by an object with waves scattered by a reference source positioned within the same plane [5–8].

However, CDI often lacks phase information, which is crucial for reconstructing object distributions. The phase distribution of the object wave needs to be recovered from the missing phases in the detector plane. This is typically accomplished using numerical iterative methods, which have some limitations:

- They rely on predefined information about the object or medium, which may not always be available or suitable.
- They involve multi-step algorithms, adding complexity and requiring more time and processing resources.

The proposed technique utilizes an array of overlapping sensors to capture scattered object waves, covering the entire observation area, including the object. Simultaneously, scattered reference waves are obtained directly from an RF signal source and/or reference sensors. This approach allows for a simpler and faster one-step algorithm for image reconstruction, using signals from overlapping sensors and reference antennas (Figure 2.6).

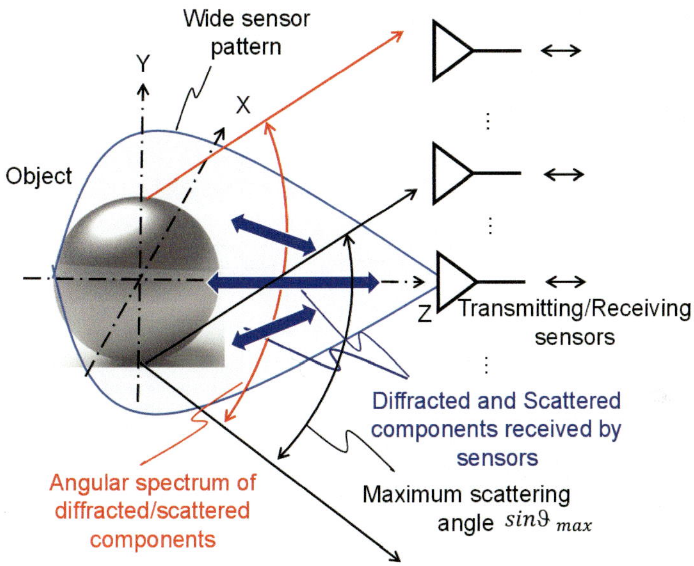

Figure 2.6 Diagram illustrating the recording of diffracted/scattered components within the Fresnel near-field region using a sensor array with wide sensor patterns.

In scenarios where coherent continuous waves illuminate an object, the resulting reflected diffracting components in the far field exhibit coherency, featuring uniform frequency and wavelength. However, due to the absence of near-field diffracted components, these far-field wavefronts do not lead to accurate shape reconstruction. Conversely, wavefronts within the near field encapsulate invaluable information concerning reflected waves, encompassing temporal and phase shifts that enable precise object shape reconstruction. Furthermore, the object's dielectric coefficient introduces a proportional phase shift for continuous waves. These additional phase shifts provide information crucial for image resolution and recognition of the object. It becomes possible to record diffracted frequency components in RF systems with wavelengths longer than the size of the object and sensors with wide numerical aperture. These components contain information about the object's size, shape, and dielectric properties. By capturing these diffracted components, RF systems can achieve high-resolution imaging and enable accurate recognition of objects, as illustrated in Figure 2.7.

Additional object information is gained by processing the digital hologram signals in various domains, such as frequency, time, and space. The spatial domain, in particular, offers valuable insights into the angular

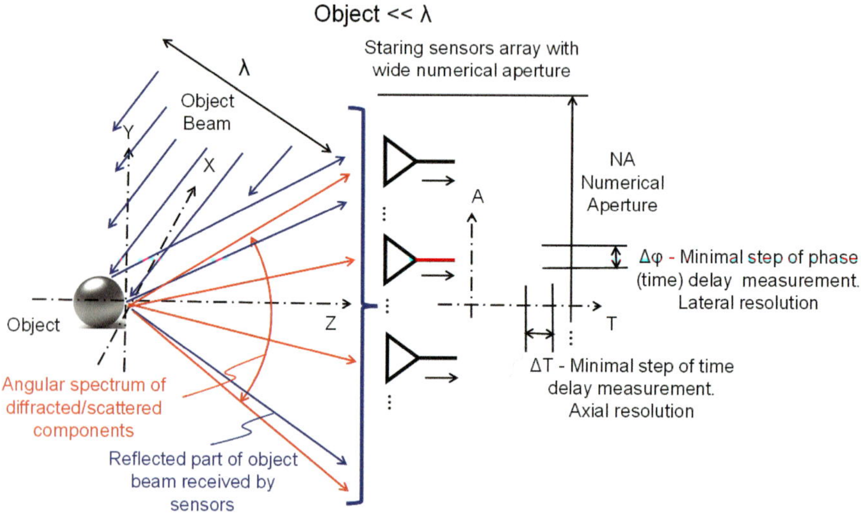

Figure 2.7 Diagram for recording scattered, reflected, and diffracted frequency components at RF frequencies in the Fresnel zone, where the wavelength is longer than the object.

distribution of scattered and diffracted components, providing object space position information by transforming the directions of signal arrival into phase or time delay measurements. Moreover, positioning receiving antennas along multiple axes offers more multi-axis information, thereby enhancing imaging resolution. By leveraging these domains and techniques, the proposed technology enables not only high-resolution imaging but also accurate object recognition across diverse applications.

2.5 Fresnel vs. Fraunhofer Diffraction

Diffraction occurs when light encounters an obstacle or aperture, causing it to bend around the edges of the obstacle. This phenomenon is particularly noticeable when the size of the obstacle or aperture is comparable to the wavelength of light. Diffraction can be categorized into two main types: near-field diffraction, also known as Fresnel diffraction, and far-field diffraction, also known as Fraunhofer diffraction (Figure 2.8). Each type of diffraction occurs under specific conditions and exhibits unique characteristics based on the distance between the light source and the diffracting object [2–4].

For Fresnel diffraction: When the light source and the screen on which the diffraction pattern is displayed are at a finite distance from the diffraction aperture the pattern observed is known as Fresnel diffraction.

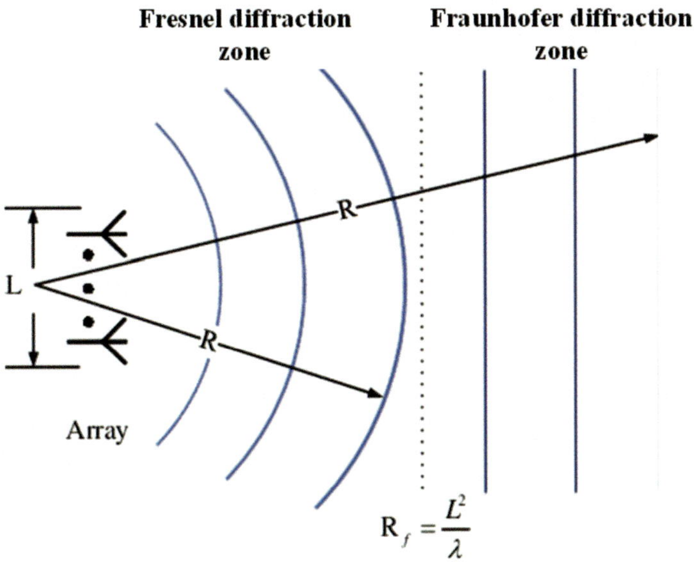

Figure 2.8 Distinguish between Fresnel and Fraunhofer diffraction.

For Fraunhofer diffraction: The source and screen are at an infinite distance from the diffracting aperture, the pattern observed is called Fraunhofer's diffraction [4] (Figure 2.9).

In optics, Fraunhofer diffraction (named after Joseph von Fraunhofer), or far-field diffraction, is a form of wave diffraction that occurs when field waves are passed through an aperture or slit causing only the size of an observed aperture image to change due to the far-field location of observation and the increasingly planar nature of outgoing diffracted waves passing through the aperture (Figure 2.9).

It is observed at distances beyond the near-field distance of Fresnel diffraction, which affects both the size and shape of the observed aperture image and occurs only when the Fresnel number $F \ll 1$, wherein the parallel rays approximation can be applied.

Fresnel diffraction or near-field diffraction is a process of diffraction that occurs when a wave passes through an aperture and diffracts in the near field, causing any diffraction pattern observed to differ in size and shape, depending on the distance between the aperture and the projection. It occurs due to the short distance in which the diffracted waves propagate, which results in a Fresnel number greater than 1 ($F > 1$). When the distance is increased, outgoing diffracted waves become planar and Fraunhofer diffraction occurs.

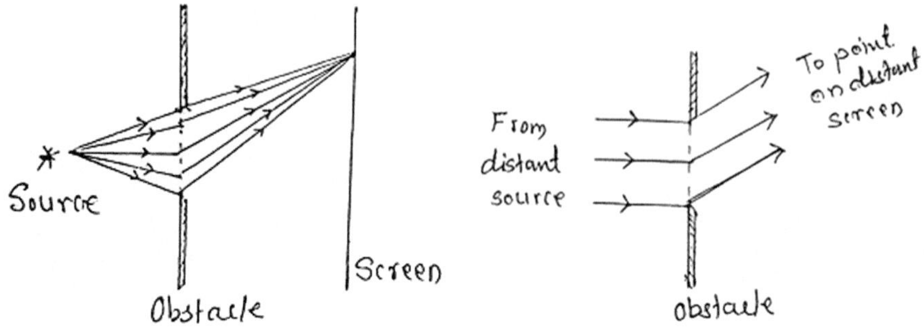

(a) (b)

Figure 2.9 Fresnel diffraction (a) when the light source and the screen on which the diffraction pattern is displayed are at a finite distance from the diffraction aperture the pattern observed is known as Fresnel diffraction. Fraunhofer diffraction (b) when the pattern observed the source and screen are at an infinite distance from the diffracting aperture. Incident and diffracted rays are parallel.

2.5.1 Near-field area criterion for RF imaging

Radio and microwave frequency waves offer superior contrast in imaging human tissues compared to X-rays, and their low power non-ionizing nature makes them a promising choice for objects recognition and biomedical imaging. Holography enables the recording of both amplitude and phase distributions of scattered waves within a single holographic record. This recorded data can then be used for numerical reconstruction, enabling retrieval of object properties such as absorption and phase shifting. When coherent continuous wave (CW) signals illuminate an object, the resulting far-field reflected signals maintain coherence with uniform frequency and wavelength, as described by the Cittert–Zernike theorem (CZT). However, the absence of near-field diffracted components within these far-field wavefronts prevents accurate reconstruction of the object's shape (Figure 2.10).

In contrast, wavefronts within the near field carry crucial information about reflected waves, including temporal and phase shifts, which are essential for precise reconstruction of the object's size and shape. Additionally, the object's dielectric coefficient introduces a phase shift proportional to the continuous wave, similar to the concept of impedance Smith chart. This additional phase and frequency shift play a pivotal role in object recognition and contribute significantly to the overall imaging process.

In RF lensless imaging within the near-field area, the criteria differ from traditional optical imaging methods. In RF diffraction imaging, the aim is

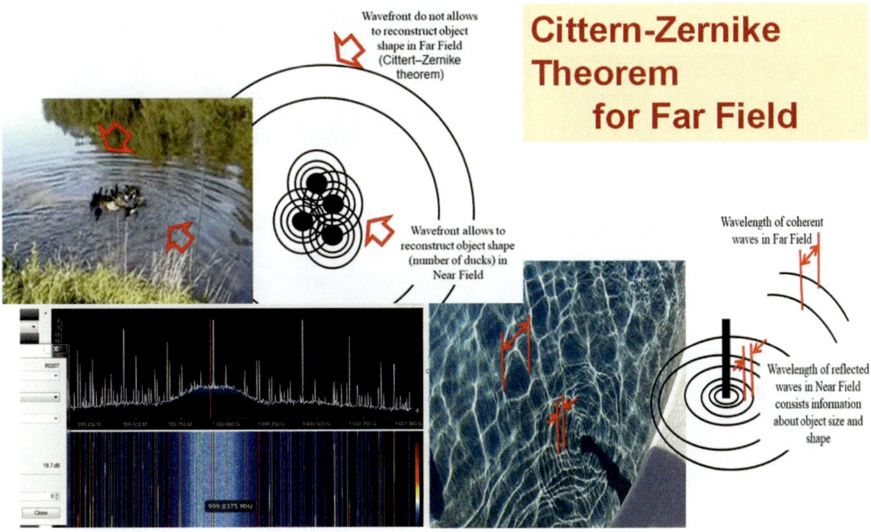

Figure 2.10 Visualization depicting wave reflection in a swimming pool, where the wavelength surpasses the object's size. Reflected diffracting components hold information about the object's form and size, measurable in the near-field zone. The extent of this area depends on both the wavelength and medium characteristics of the applied waves. Importantly, the size of the near-field region can exceed a few wavelengths.

to capture the highest possible orders of diffracted waves to achieve optimal image resolution. To achieve this goal, it's crucial to consider the properties of the medium through which RF waves propagate, including its absorption characteristics. Defining the near-field and far-field areas is influenced not only by the size and design of the antenna elements but also by the medium's viscosity and its physical resistance to RF wave propagation and scattering.

The transformation of reflected time-space domain signals into the frequency domain allows for the filtering of frequency components containing vital information about the object's shape, size, and dielectric coefficient. This transformation generates a spectrum signature unique to the object under observation. Notably, the diffraction of continuous waves produces additional frequency components corresponding to the object's size and shape in the near field. Unlike harmonics, these frequency components typically fall within the 5%–20% range relative to the transmitting frequency, as illustrated in Figure 2.11.

The near-field area in RF wavefront imaging is characterized by the region where multiple diffracted phase- and frequency-shifted components can still

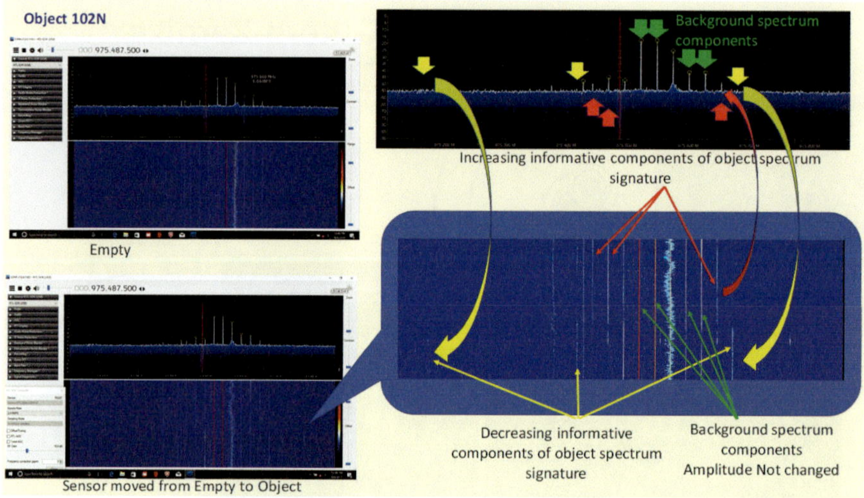

Figure 2.11 Spectrum signature of the object with scattering medium (background spectrum components). Antenna moving from empty zone to zone with object. Object components are growing, background components are not changing.

be reliably detected and measured. This determination of the near-field is influenced by various factors, including the properties of the medium through which the waves propagate. By taking into account the absorption properties of the medium and how they affect wave behaviors, RF wavefront imaging can offer a distinctive and efficient approach to achieving high-resolution imaging. This understanding allows for precise delineation of the near-field region, where the complex interplay of diffracted components can be leveraged to extract detailed information about the object under observation.

2.6 Resolution of Staring Sensor Array with Wide Numerical Aperture

This section describes the resolution of reconstructed images when a staring sensor array with a wide numerical aperture is applied.

2.6.1 Abbe resolution criterion for optical systems

In the context of high-scattering mediums, the scattering of laser signals is characterized by the maximum scattering angle, where only a fraction of the components reflected from the object are received by a narrow-beam sensor. According to the Abbe criterion, the smallest resolvable object must be larger than half a wavelength. The mathematical equation for lateral resolution [9–11]:

$$R_{\text{Lateral}}^{\text{Abbe}} = \frac{\lambda}{2n\sin\vartheta_{\max}} = \frac{\lambda}{2NA}, \tag{2.1}$$

where:

$\sin\vartheta_{\max}$ – the maximal scattering angle detected by the optical system, n – is the refractive index,

$NA = n\sin\vartheta_{\max}$ – the numerical aperture of the system.

For $n = 1$ in the following, $NA \approx a/z$, where z is the distance from the aperture,

a – the radius of the aperture for the optical system.

Scanning objects with a narrow beam fails to capture a sufficient part of the diffraction pattern and angular distribution of the diffracted and scattered components reflected from the object (Figure 2.12). As a result, a significant amount of information about the object is lost. In such systems, the positioning accuracy and image resolution are determined by the beam width of the receiving sensor. Although using shorter wavelength signals can enhance accuracy, it is constrained by the increasing scattering and absorption in the medium. This limitation hinders the effectiveness of narrow beam scanning in achieving high-resolution imaging and comprehensive object recognition.

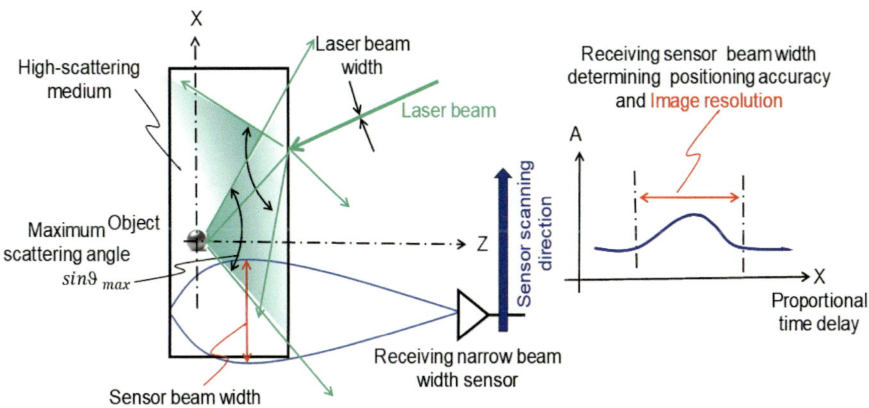

Figure 2.12 Laser-based object detection system with scanning narrow beam receiving sensor. Image resolution is determined by receiving sensor beam width.

2.6.2 Resolution for RF systems

Low-power radiofrequency/microwave signals have better-penetrating capability through high-scattering mediums, and more diffracted and scattered components, which characterize objects and medium can be received by a wide angular aperture sensor (Figure 2.13). The Abbe resolution for radiofrequency (RF) diffraction imaging system is defined as:

$$R^{\text{RF}}_{\text{Lateral}} = \frac{\lambda}{2NA}, \tag{2.2}$$

where:

λ– the applied RF wavelength,

$NA = x/a$ – the numerical aperture of the RF wide angular aperture sensor equal to the number of minimal steps of phase measurement in the aperture of the RF antenna by axis X,

a – the size of the minimum step of phase difference measurement with one RF antenna along axis X,

x – the aperture size of RF antenna by axis X,

$\sin\vartheta_{\text{max}}$ – the maximal scattering angle for RF.

Therefore, lateral resolution in RF systems is inversely proportional to the numerical aperture (*NA*), which corresponds to the number of minimum phase measurement steps in the antenna aperture along the X-axis. A larger numerical aperture leads to better lateral resolution.

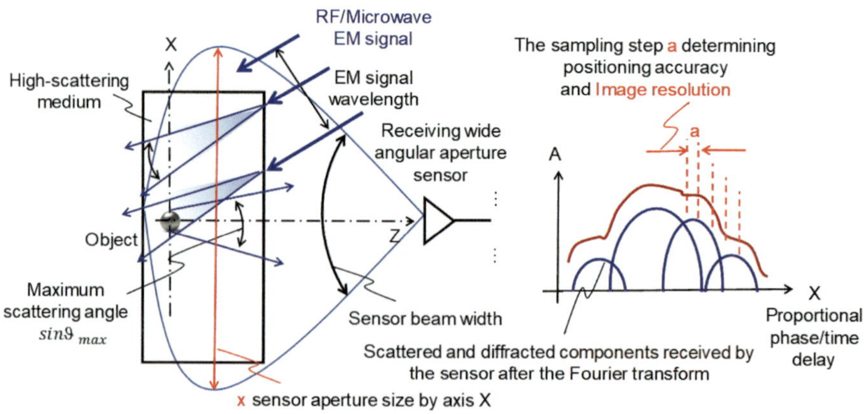

Figure 2.13 RF/microwave long wavelength signals have better penetrating capability through high-scattering mediums, and more diffracted and scattered components, which characterize objects and medium can be received by wide-aperture sensors.

The axial resolution in RF imaging is inversely proportional to the square of the numerical aperture, which corresponds to the numerical aperture $NA = z/\Delta z'$ – the axial resolution of the RF system, which is the step of axial phase control for by Z-axis RF system. This means that increasing the numerical aperture significantly improves axial resolution.

The numerical aperture (NA) of an RF imaging system can be increased in two primary ways:

1. Increasing the size of the antenna or creating an antenna array. A larger antenna size can capture more diffracted components, thereby improving the resolution. Using multiple antennas arranged in an array can effectively increase the numerical aperture, capturing more comprehensive diffraction patterns.
2. Decreasing the minimal phase measurement steps. Increasing the RF signal's sampling frequency allows for finer phase measurements. Ensuring the stability of frequency and phase measurements enhances the system's ability to resolve fine details.

In the proposed technology, staring sensors with wide numerical apertures offer significant advantages:

1. Simultaneous information capture. These sensors provide simultaneous information about the entire object, enabling comprehensive data collection without the need for scanning.
2. Recording diffraction patterns. The wide numerical aperture allows for the recording of diffraction patterns for each point on the object and their angular distribution within the Fresnel zone.
3. Improved measurement accuracy. The accuracy of measurements in orthogonal or multi-axis directions is crucial for determining imaging resolution. The ability to capture detailed phase and amplitude information from multiple directions enhances the overall resolution and accuracy of the imaging system.

By leveraging these techniques, the proposed RF imaging technology can achieve higher resolution and more accurate object recognition, making it effective for a wide range of applications [9–11].

The proposed technology for RF wavefront coherent diffraction imaging offers several key advantages by enhancing imaging resolution in RF wavefront coherent diffraction imaging. Fundamentally altering how resolution is determined compared to traditional methods. The key features of the proposed technology:

- Resolution beyond the spatial diffraction limit. Unlike traditional spatial diffraction-limited systems, the imaging resolution here is determined by the digitizing sampling frequency or the minimum step of phase measurement. This key feature enables high-resolution imaging beyond conventional spatial limitations.
- Wide numerical aperture sensors. The sensors or antennas with wide numerical apertures are designed to receive diffracted components reflected from all scattering points of the entire object, capturing comprehensive diffraction patterns.

Key takeaways from eqn (2.1) and (2.2) for RF wavefront coherent diffraction imaging:

1. Resolution and wavelength:
    - Both lateral and axial resolutions in RF imaging are directly proportional to the wavelength of the applied RF signals. While shorter wavelengths provide higher resolution, the proposed Fresnel coherent diffraction imaging technique can enhance resolution by several orders of magnitude.
    - Lateral resolution and numerical aperture. The lateral resolution in RF imaging is inversely proportional to the numerical aperture (NA) of the RF system. This corresponds to the number of minimum phase measurement steps in the antenna array aperture along the X or Y axis. A larger numerical aperture results in better lateral resolution.
    - Axial resolution and numerical aperture. The axial resolution in RF imaging is inversely proportional to the square of the numerical aperture. The numerical aperture for axial resolution, $NA = z/\Delta z'$, represents the step of axial phase control along the Z-axis. Increasing the numerical aperture significantly improves axial resolution.
2. Increasing numerical aperture for RF imaging systems:
    - Antenna array size. Increasing the size of the antenna array, although limited by the maximum size of scattered signals from the object.
    - Minimal phase measurement steps. Decreasing the minimal phase measurement steps by enhancing RF signal sampling frequency and stability.
    - Wide aperture antennas. Utilizing wide aperture antennas without increasing the physical size of the antenna, which imposes stricter

requirements on the transmitter and sampling frequency and phase stability.

3. Minimal phase measurement steps:
   - The smallest phase measurement step in the RF system is analogous to the pixel size in optical systems. This resolution criterion is fundamental for optimizing and interpreting RF wavefront imaging, ensuring accurate and detailed visualization.

The proposed digital holographic processing technique provides limitless scalable resolution determined by the sampling frequency. This innovative approach enables high-resolution imaging by leveraging wide numerical aperture sensors and advanced RF signal processing methods. It offers significant improvements in both lateral and axial resolution, paving the way for precise and detailed imaging across various applications.

2.7 Development of High-resolution RF Imaging System

2.7.1 Recording of high-resolution digital hologram for image reconstruction

The optical setup for recording holograms, as traditionally described in resources such as the Encyclopedia Britannica, provides a foundational understanding of holography. In this setup, holograms are recorded on photographic plates, as depicted in Figure 2.14. The holography concept is unique in that every segment of a hologram contains the complete image of the object. This means that even if a corner of the hologram is cut off, the entire image can still be observed through the remaining piece.

The complete hologram and a cutout segment both encapsulate information about the entire object, as illustrated in Figure 2.15. Two crucial implications arise from the nature of holograms:

- Inherent information: Each segment of the recorded hologram inherently conveys viewpoint information about the entire object, aligning with the fundamental concept of a "hologram."
- Quality enhancement: The quality of the image reconstructed from the entire or a substantial part of the hologram surpasses that reconstructed from a small fragment.

Image reconstruction is commonly performed numerically using digitized interferograms. Digital holography leverages measured optical phase data and frequently yields three-dimensional images. A set of holograms recorded from various directions or with different reference wave orientations enables

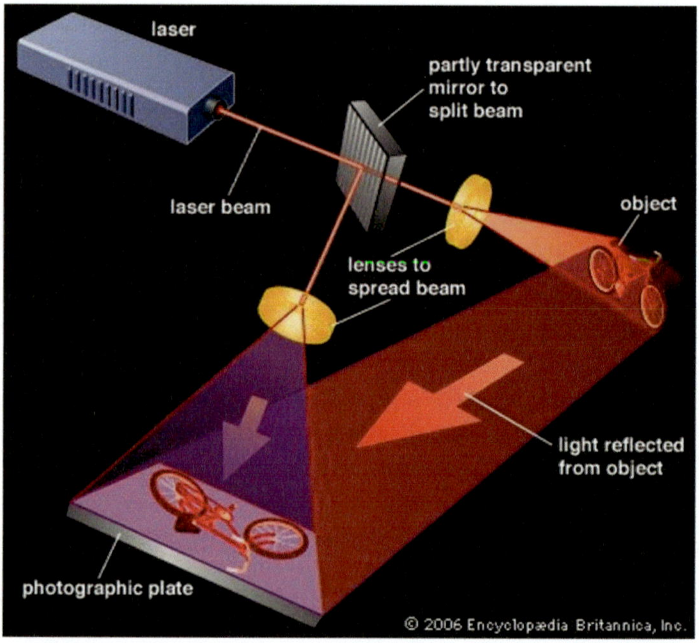

Figure 2.14 Setup for recording hologram by laser beam on photographic plate published in Encyclopedia Britannica.

numerical emulation of an object with a large numerical aperture, resulting in enhanced resolution [12–15].

The integration of orbital angular momentum lattice (OAML) to holography showcases the practical feasibility of multiplexed holography across multiple dimensions, opening up new possibilities for the advancement of practical information encryption systems [11]. Utilizing anisotropic metamaterial platforms for local control of polarization in complex vector beams, tailoring optical field topologies through plasmonics, and harnessing complex light beams with intricate polarization, along with microsphere-assisted imaging, hold promise for achieving higher-resolution imaging in various photonic and quantum technologies, as well as in applications such as imaging and metrology.

Digital holography typically involves acquiring and processing holograms using a digital sensor array, commonly a CCD camera (charge-coupled device) or a similar device. The resolution of CCD cameras faces limitations imposed by the minimal size of the detector or pixel, restricted by the smallest detected or imaging wavelength, known as the diffraction limit.

As illustrated in Figure 2.16, a CCD camera's imaging detector records signal intensity in each separate detector, generating a regular image rather than a hologram. While recorded images or corresponding digital signals may contain phases if used for analog or digital reference, individual pieces of

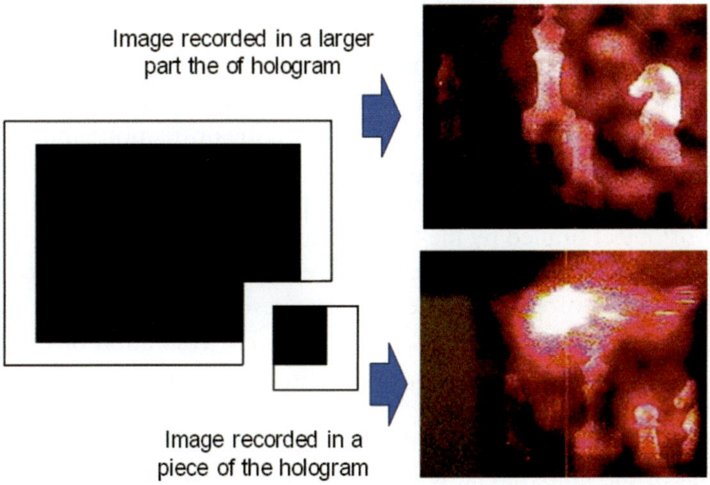

Figure 2.15 The full hologram and a piece of the hologram containing information about the entire object.

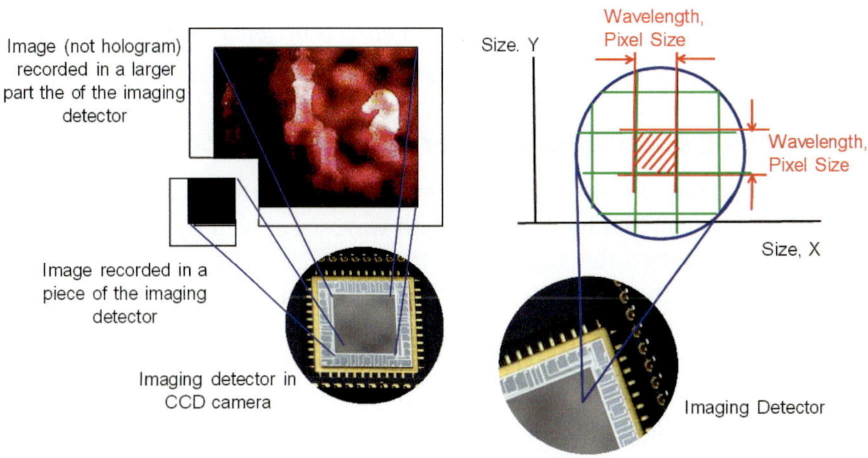

Figure 2.16 Resolution of the image recorded with a CCD camera, constrained by pixel size. The minimal pixel size is limited by the smallest detected or imaging wavelength, or diffraction limit.

recorded images lack information about the entire object. In this scenario, minimal imaging resolution is determined by the geometrical size of the smallest detector and pixel. Efforts to enhance holographic imaging resolution involve recording techniques that combine digital holograms, similar to interferometric microscopy. The digital analysis of a set of holograms recorded from different directions or with different reference wave orientations allows numerical emulation of an object with a large numerical aperture, thereby improving resolution correspondingly. However, the image resolution remains constrained by the minimal size of the detector or pixel, limited by the smallest detected or imaging wavelength, i.e., the diffraction limit.

The imaging detector in the CCD camera (Figure 2.16) is recording light intensity in some spots of the object. Each recording pixel presents some spatial spot of object limited by the field of view of one CCD camera sensor. Camera does not allows to record scattered, reflected or diffract components out of field of view of each one sensor. The resolution of imaging CCD cameras is limited by the smallest size of pixel. The resolution of imaging CCD cameras is limited by the smallest size of pixel, which limits of detecting signals wavelength.

The staring sensor array with wide numerical apertures not only enables the recording of the holographic matrix of the object but also addresses the diffraction limit challenge. This technology shifts the resolution limit from the spatial domain (minimal pixel size approximately equal to the wavelength) to the time domain (minimal sampling/digitizing signal wavelength or minimal step of phase measurement), which can be tens of thousands of times smaller than using the object wavelength, as illustrated in Figure 2.17.

2.7.2 Resolving phase ambiguity for digital diffraction pattern

Image reconstruction techniques in holography usually involve the superimposition of waves scattered by an object with waves scattered by a reference source positioned within the same plane [5]. Coherent diffraction imaging (CDI) can achieve high-resolution results by capturing high-order diffraction components [6–8]. However, CDI often lacks phase information, which is crucial for reconstructing object distributions. Fourier transform holography (FTH) is another imaging technique where object waves are combined with reference waves within the same plane, solving the phase problem and enabling the acquisition of high-resolution data (Figure 2.18).

This configuration allows for a simpler and faster algorithm for image reconstruction compared to traditional methods. The use of an array of

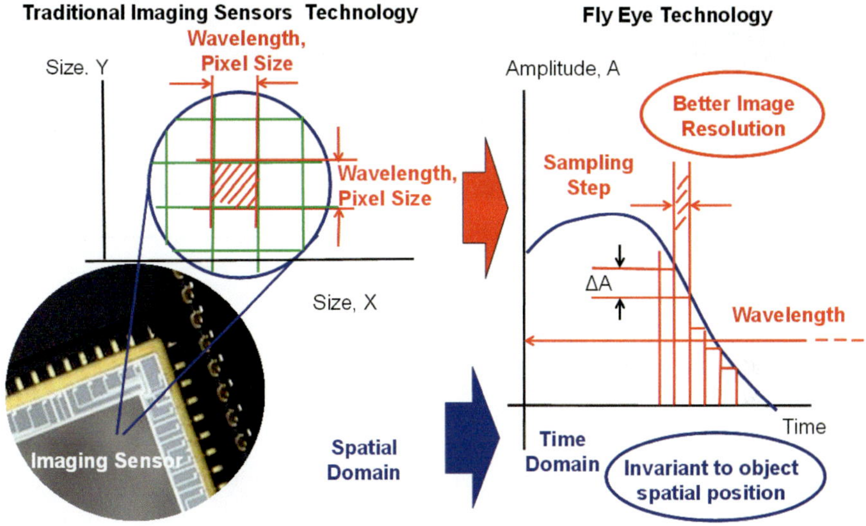

Figure 2.17 New digital holographic technology shifts the resolution limit from the spatial domain (minimal pixel size approximately equal to the wavelength) to the time domain (minimal sampling/digitizing signal wavelength or minimal step of phase measurement). Theoretically limitless imaging resolution will be limited now by highest sampling frequency corresponding to the minimal step of phase measurement, and transmitting signal and synchronization signals frequency/phase stability.

sensors with overlapping patterns ensures comprehensive coverage of the object and its surroundings.

Direct detection and digitizing of signals provide a few advances:

- Real-time measurement of amplitudes, phases, and angular distribution of diffraction patterns relative to processor time for recording digital holographic matrix.
- Direct digitizing allows to use digital interface to transfer real-time amplitudes and phases information to processor and forming digital hologram practically without losses because digital interface ability to recovering transferring digital information.
- Direct detection and digitizing of signals allow the distribution of antennas without losing information of amplitude and phase [17, 18].

The recorded digital holographic matrix contains information about the object's distribution pattern, and the real-time nature of the process facilitates efficient data processing. Therefore, RF holographic imaging can be applied

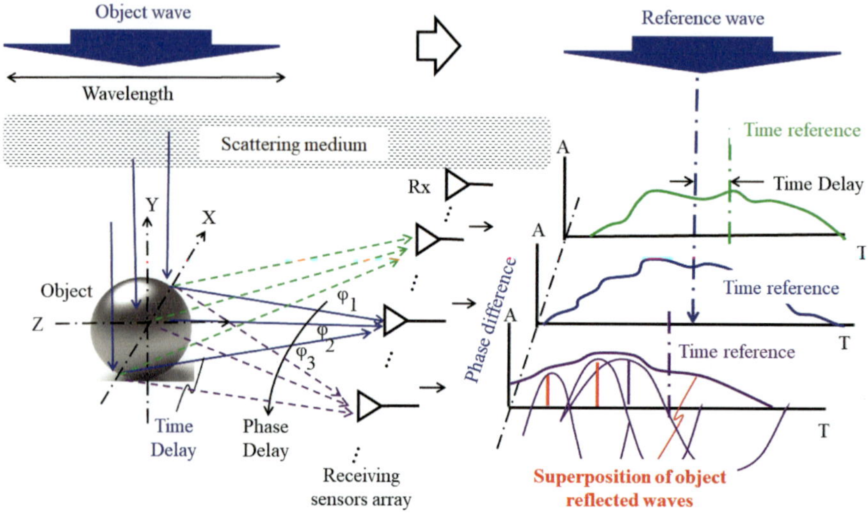

Figure 2.18 Lack of phase information, which is crucial for reconstructing object distributions is compensated by using reference beam signals. This Fourier transform holography imaging technique is where object waves are combined with reference waves within the same plane, solving the phase problem and enabling the acquisition of high-resolution data.

to create high-resolution digital holograms. Therefore, digital holographic recording provides:

- In RF wavefront imaging, the holographic recording and direct digitized, allowing for the capture of detailed phase and amplitude information of scattered and diffracted waves.
- Utilizing sensors with a wide numerical aperture ensures that diffracted components from all scattering points of the object are captured. This comprehensive data collection is critical for accurate image reconstruction.
- The recorded digital holograms can be processed to reconstruct high-resolution images of the object. This involves transforming the captured phase and amplitude data into a visual representation of the object, taking advantage of the holographic property where each segment contains the whole image information.

The recording of high-resolution digital holograms using the principles of traditional holography, but applied to RF wavefront imaging, offers significant advantages. By capturing comprehensive diffraction patterns and utilizing the unique properties of holography, this method enables the reconstruction of detailed and accurate images. The ability to view the entire image from various angles and perspectives ensures that critical information about the object's size, shape, and properties is preserved, facilitating high-resolution imaging across diverse applications.

2.8 Design of Staring Antenna Arrays for High-resolution Imaging

For achieving high-resolution RF imaging, an antenna array must be designed to encompass a wide observation area, capturing all objects of interest and providing detailed information about them. A novel and effective approach to this is the use of a staring antenna array. A staring antenna array is characterized by multiple static receiving antenna beams that remain fixed and continuously gather information. This continuous, uninterrupted data collection stands in stark contrast to scanning radars, where the transmitted beam sweeps across the scene.

Staring antenna arrays provide:

1. Unlike scanning radars, staring antenna arrays use a stationary transmitted/received flood beam that can encompass multiple static receiver beams. This arrangement significantly enhances reception gain and the accuracy of angle localization.
2. By providing a continuous stream of data, staring antenna arrays deliver comprehensive information necessary for optimal object detection, localization, and identification. This continuous data collection ensures no interruption, which is crucial for high-resolution imaging.
3. Staring radars can adjust processing dwell time or employ multiple parallel processes, each with its own processing dwell time. This capability ensures time-efficient detection and is unattainable in mechanically scanned surveillance radars or conventional phased array radars.

To achieve high accuracy in direction finding, a well-designed antenna array is essential. Lipsky S.E. proposed an innovative solution involving an array of fixed, narrow beamwidth antennas oriented to provide omnidirectional coverage. These antennas are strategically positioned to cover all directions, ensuring comprehensive and precise angle measurements. By selecting appropriate antennas, the system can facilitate accurate microwave direction finding. He proposed monopulse method processing utilizing pairs of directional antennas positioned by azimuth and elevation boresight. The monopulse technique allows for precise direction finding by comparing the signals received from these pairs of antennas.

The staring antenna array approach offers significant advantages over traditional scanning radars, particularly in the context of high-resolution RF imaging. By utilizing static receiver beams and a stationary transmitted beam, staring arrays provide continuous, comprehensive data collection, enabling precise object detection, localization, and identification. Additionally, implementing the monopulse method for high-accuracy direction finding further enhances the system's capability, making it a robust solution for various RF imaging applications [16] (Figure 2.19).

The integration of the staring antenna array with the high-accuracy monopulse method and digital processing and synchronization is a key feature of the "Fly Eye Radar Concept." This innovative approach significantly enhances imaging resolution and provides detailed object information, making it a robust solution for high-resolution RF imaging:

1. The antenna array consists of directional antennas with overlapping patterns in multiple axes. This configuration enhances imaging resolution and allows for the collection of additional object information.
2. Monopulse processing improves accuracy in direction finding and phase delay measurement. This method involves comparing signals received from pairs of directional antennas positioned by azimuth and elevation boresight. Overlapping antenna patterns, illustrated in polar coordinates, demonstrate the effectiveness of monopulse processing in achieving precise direction finding.

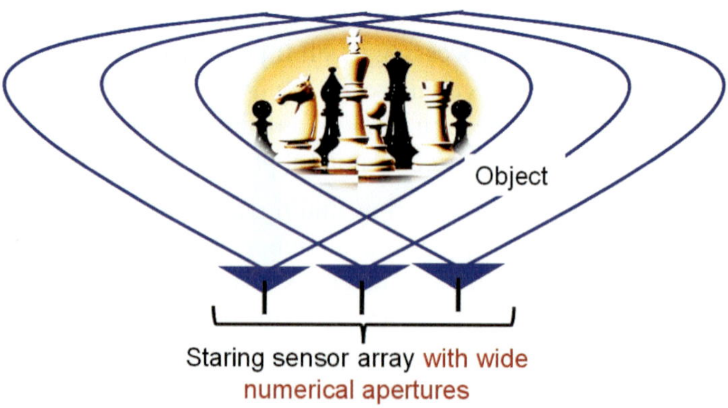

Figure 2.19 Wide numerical aperture antennas must cover the entire object or area of possible object observation.

3. Advanced digital processing techniques and synchronization mechanisms are employed to handle the data collected by the antenna arrays. This ensures accurate and efficient processing of the RF signals.

For effective RF diffraction imaging, it is essential to record digital holograms that capture the complete diffraction patterns of the objects of interest. This requires comprehensive coverage of the entire observation area, which can be challenging with traditional scanning systems. Multiple antenna arrays positioned along multiple axes ensure that the entire object or observation area is covered. This approach overcomes the limitations of traditional scanning systems with narrow beams, which might miss signals reflected outside the antenna's field of view.

A planar antenna array configuration, as exemplified in Figure 2.20, is particularly suitable for capturing RF diffraction imaging holograms of wide observation areas. This setup allows for the simultaneous recording of scattered and diffracted signals from multiple points on the object.

The integration of staring antenna arrays, high-accuracy monopulse processing, and advanced digital synchronization within the "Fly Eye Radar Concept" offers significant improvements in RF imaging resolution. By ensuring comprehensive coverage and precise direction finding, this approach enables the recording of high-resolution digital holograms for RF diffraction imaging. The planar antenna array configuration further enhances the capability to capture detailed diffraction patterns, making this technology highly effective for a wide range of applications in RF imaging.

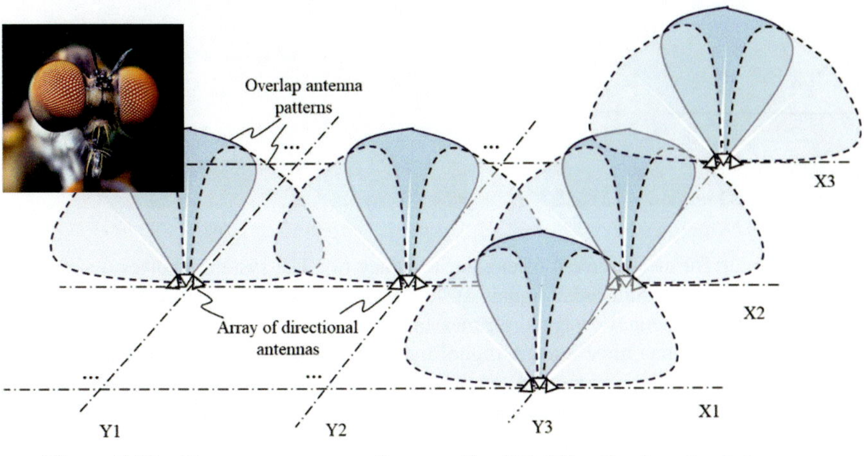

Figure 2.20 Planar antenna array for recording RF diffraction imaging hologram.

This innovative approach to antenna array design and implementation holds substantial potential for high-resolution RF imaging applications, offering a new dimension of accuracy and information gathering.

2.9 Measurement of Imaging Resolution

Elements of setup for the measurement of directional and axial accuracy at different frequencies are depicted in Figure 2.21.

The measurements conducted at different frequencies have demonstrated a high level of consistency in terms of angular, axial, and lateral accuracy. This consistent accuracy is crucial for the reliability and effectiveness of RF imaging technology across various applications.

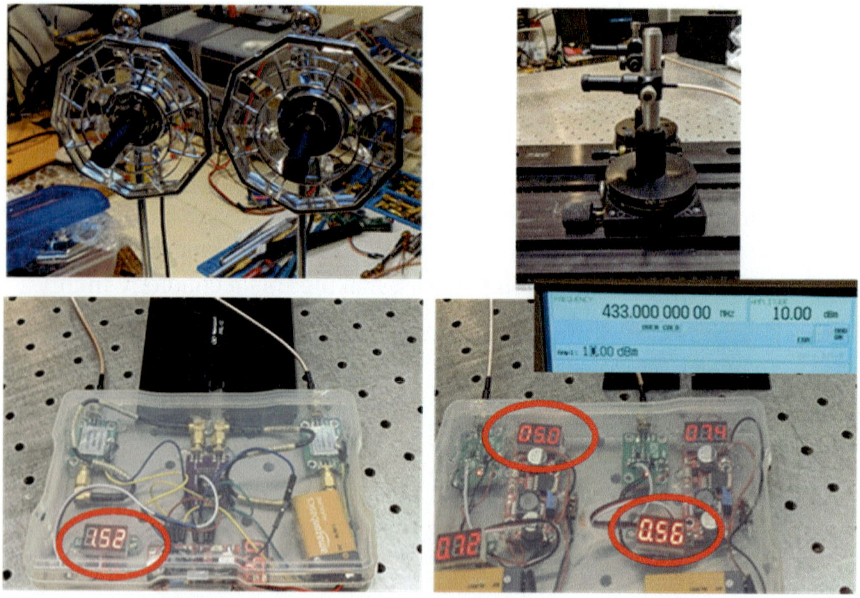

(a) (b)

Figure 2.21 Setup for measurement of angular accuracy (a). The system involves a signal generator transmitting the sinusoidal signals at 433 MHz frequency. The receiving circuit comprises two overlap antennas designed for measuring the direction angle by observing the phase shift between antenna directions. A digital indicator is calibrated in angular degrees. Setup for measurement axial accuracy (b) comprises two antennas configurated to measure different distances between each antenna and signal generator. Digital indicators calibrated in millimeters facilitate accurate axial measurement.

Key measurement results:

1. Transmitting signal frequency of 433 MHz:
   - Wavelength: 692 mm
   - Angular accuracy: Minimal measured angular shift between directions of antennas: 2 degrees.
   - This results in a directional accuracy of approximately 0.0055 times the wavelength.
2. Axial accuracy:
   - Minimal detected axial shift between antennas: 3 mm.
   - This indicates an axial accuracy of approximately 0.0043 times the wavelength.

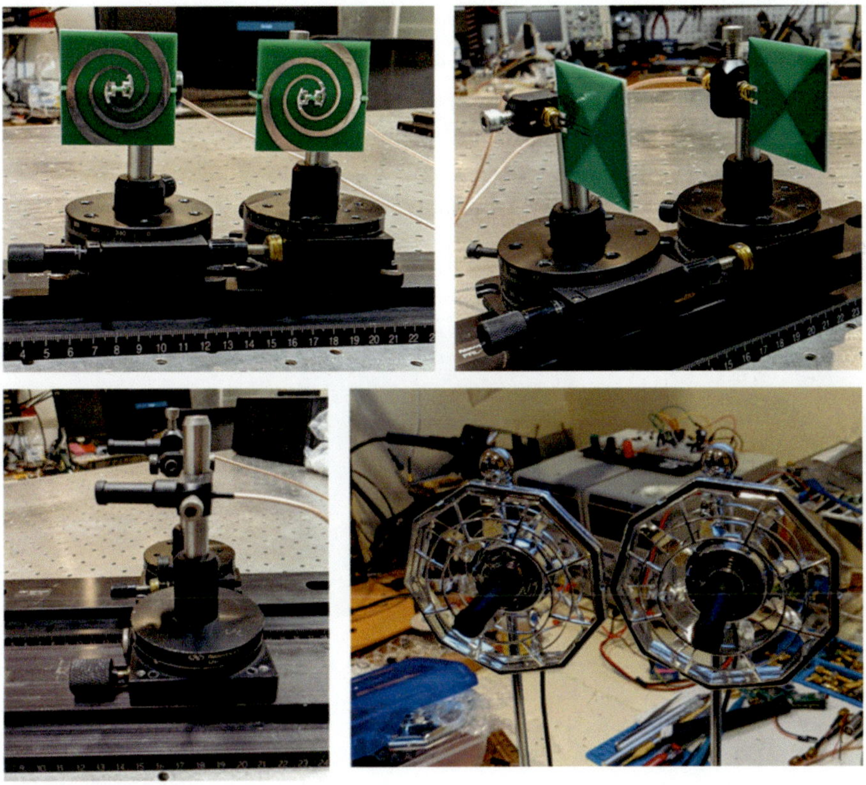

Figure 2.22 Directional antennas for different frequency bands used for directional and axial accuracy measurements.

3. Consistency across frequencies:
   - These measurements were conducted across various frequencies, and similar levels of accuracy were observed. The consistency in angular, axial, and lateral measurements showcases the robustness of the technology.
4. Frequency bands tested:
   - 2.4–5.8 GHz band:
     Directional, lateral, and axial measurements were consistent and reliable.
   - 2.4–10.5 GHz band:
     Consistent accuracy was also observed in this broader frequency range.
   - 433 MHz band:
     As noted above, specific measurements at 433 MHz demonstrated the technology's effectiveness at lower frequencies as well.

Figure 2.22 presents the images of the antennas used for directional, lateral, and axial measurements within the specified frequency bands (2.4–5.8 GHz, 2.4–10.5 GHz, and 433 MHz). The visual representation reinforces the consistency and reliability of the measurements across different frequency ranges.

Figure 2.23 Fly Eye antenna arrays designed by AMPAC Science Inc, Cobham Inc, and PMI Inc. for different applications. Directional antenna arrays were distributed around the perimeter of small and micro UAVs for sense and avoid systems.

Directional antenna arrays can be designed for different applications and can have analog or digital interface and corresponding output signals connectors. The application of directional antenna arrays distributed on small and nano UAV for sense and avoid applications is shown in Figure 2.23.

Conclusion

The novel vision technology's ability to provide consistent and reliable accuracy across different frequency ranges is a significant advantage. The demonstrated angular, axial, and lateral accuracies at various frequencies underscore the robustness and versatility of the RF imaging system. These findings suggest that the technology is well-suited for a wide range of applications, offering dependable performance in diverse operational environments.

The minimal measured angular, lateral, and axial accuracy observed between two antenna positions or points indicates that signals reflected from these object points can be measured with the same angular, lateral, and axial accuracy. This precision can then be utilized for object image reconstruction. The measurements affirm that the provided technology allows for image reconstruction with an accuracy approximately 1000 times smaller than the wavelength.

An essential implication of these measurements is the revelation that the reconstructed image resolution is not directly constrained by the wavelength. This departure from the traditional diffraction limit suggests that long wavelengths, such as radio frequency electromagnetic waves known for their good penetration through obstacles like walls, ground, and the human body, can be effectively employed for creating high-resolution imaging. This highlights the potential of the proposed technology to overcome the limitations associated with the diffraction limit, enabling high-resolution imaging and object recognition in various challenging environments.

References

[1] Imaging Resolution, Wikipedia. [Online], Available www.wikipedia.org [Accessed April 20, 2024].

[2] C. *Thomas, T. Ranchin, L. Wald, J. Chanussot,* "Synthesis of multispectral images to high spatial resolution: a critical review of fusion methods based on remote sensing physics," *IEEE Transactions on Geoscience and Remote Sensing. 46 (5): 13011312,2007.*

[3] G. Scientist, "Distinguish Between Fresnel and Fraunhofer Diffraction," [Online] Available https://gkscientist.com [Accessed Jul 26, 2023].

[4] "MASSACHUSETTS INSTITUTE OF TECHNOLOGY" Chapter 14, Interference and Diffraction. [Online] Available https://mit.edu [Accessed May, 01, 2023].

[5] S. Mustafi, Tatiana Latychevskaia, "Fourier Transform Holography: A Lensless Imaging Technique," Photonics 2023, 10, 153, [Online] Available https://www.mdpi.com/journal/photonics [Accessed May 01.2023].

[6] T. Latychevskaia, "Lateral and axial resolution criteria in incoherent and coherent optics and holography, near- and far-field regimes," Opt. Express, 2023.

[7] T. Latychevskaia, J.-N. Longchamp, and H.-W. Fink, "When holography meets coherent diffraction imaging," Opt. Express 20, 28871–28892, 2012.

[8] T. Latychevskaia," Iterative phase retrieval in coherent diffractive imaging: practical issues," Applied Optics, September 2018, [Online], Available https://www.researchgate.net/publication/327210662 [Accessed May,01,2023].

[9] E. Abbe, "The relation of aperture and power in the microscope," Journal of the Royal Microscopical Society 2, 300–309, 1882.

[10] L. Rayleigh, "Investigations in optics, with special reference to the spectroscope" . Physics, Royal Astronomical Society, Published 1 February, 1880.

[11] X. Yang, H. Mei, J. Zhang, K. Xu, B. Yin, Q. Zhang, and X. Wei, "Drfn: Deep recurrent fusion network for single-image super-resolution with large factors," IEEE Transactions on Multimedia, vol. 21, no. 2, pp. 328–337, 2018.

[12] K. Prajapati, V. Chudasama, H. Patel, A. Sarvaiya, K. P. Upla, K. Raja, R. Ramachandra, and C. Busch, "Channel split convolutional neural network (chasnet) for thermal image super-resolution," Proceedings of the IEEE/CVF Conference on Computer Vision and Pattern Recognition, 2021, pp. 4368–4377.

[13] Y. Zhang, K. Li, K. Li, L. Wang, B. Zhong, and Y. Fu, "Image super-resolution using very deep residual channel attention networks," in Proceedings of the European conference on computer vision (ECCV), 2018, pp. 286–301.

[14] B. Niu, W. Wen, W. Ren, X. Zhang, L. Yang, S. Wang, K. Zhang, X. Cao, and H. Shen, "Single image super-resolution via a holistic attention network," in European Conference on Computer Vision. Springer, 2020, pp. 191–207.

[15] A. Yang, B. Yang, Z. Ji, Y. Pang, and L. Shao, "Lightweight group convolutional network for single image super-resolution," Information Sciences, vol. 516, pp. 220–233, 2020.

[16] S. Lipsky, "Microwave passive direction finder," SciTech Publishing Inc. Raleigh, NC 27613, 2004.

[17] M. Kappes, S. Norsworthy, "Why Direct RF Sampling is a Game Changer," March 2023. IQ-Analog Corporation, 12348 High Bluff Drive, San Diego, California, U.S.A. 92130, [Online] Available www.iq analog.com [Accessed April 20, 2024].

[18] F. Deviere, N. Seller and J. Rohou, "Making history: advanced system in a package technology enable direct RF conversion," White paper, Microwave Journal, Vol. 64, No. 1, January 2021.

[19] Y. Kuznetsova, A. Neumann, S. R. Brueck, "Imaging interferometric microscopy–approaching the linear systems limits of optical resolution," Optics Express. 15 (11): 6651–6663. Bibcode: PMID 19546975, 2007.

[20] M. Paturzo; F. Merola; S. Grilli; S. De Nicola; A. Finizio; P. Ferraro. "Super-resolution in digital holography by a two-dimensional dynamic phase grating," Optics Express. 16 (21): PMID 18852822, 2008.

[21] Tian Xia, Zhenwei Xie, Xiaocong Yuan, "Multidimensional multiplexing holography based on optical orbital angular momentum lattice multiplexing," Advanced Photonics Nexus, Vol. 3, Issue 1, 016005, January 2024. [Online] Available https://doi.org/10.1117/1.APN.3.1.016005 [Acessed April 20, 2024].

[22] Chu Xu, Tianyu Yang, Pengxin Zou, and Ran Ye "Photonic-hook enhanced microsphere-assisted label-free super-resolution imaging," Proc. SPIE 12316, Advanced Optical Imaging Technologies V, 1231602, 30 December 2022. [Online] Available https://doi.org/10.1 117/12.2642931 [Accessed April 20, 2024].

[23] V, Aita, D. Roth, A.Bykov, A. V. Zayats, "Tailoring optical field topologies with plasmonics and metamaterials," SPIE, Vol. Proc. SPIE PC12197, Plasmonics: Design, Materials, Fabrication, Characterization, and Applications XX, PC121970L.

[24] Zhen Liu, Decang Bi, Weibiao Chen, Jiqiao Liu, and Xiaopeng Zhu "Antenna efficiency and aperture optimization analysis of spaceborne coherent wind lidar," Proc. SPIE 12706, First International Conference on Spatial Atmospheric Marine Environmental Optics (SAME 2023), 127060E, 24 May 2023. [Online] Available https://doi.org/10.1117/12 .2681978 [Accessed April 20, 2023].

3

Objects Recognition in High-scattering Medium at Radio/Microwave Frequencies

Introduction

Radio and microwave electromagnetic waves are widely recognized for their exceptional ability to penetrate diverse mediums such as human tissues, walls, and ground surfaces, while posing low risks of ionizing radiation. This inherent capability makes them highly advantageous for various imaging applications. However, achieving high-resolution imaging and precise object recognition in environments characterized by high scattering poses a formidable challenge.

To address these challenges, a novel technique is proposed for object recognition in high-scattering mediums, leveraging spectrum signatures within the radio/microwave frequency ranges. This approach integrates the angular spectrum of diffracted and scattered components into Fresnel coherent diffraction imaging (FCDI) for digitally recording object distribution patterns. Unlike traditional imaging methods constrained by minimum pixel size limitations, digital holography in this technique ensures that the minimum resolution is determined by the precision of digital sampling steps. This characteristic remains invariant despite the relatively long wavelengths of radio and microwave frequencies.

The proposed technique involves Fourier transforming and filtering the distribution of diffracting components received from overlapping and reference antennas. This process allows for the separation of objects from the medium based on their spectral signatures. The diffraction components provide valuable insights into the object's dielectric properties, size, and shape. Importantly, these characteristics remain invariant to the object's spatial position.

This technique represents a significant advancement in object recognition within challenging high-scattering mediums at radio and microwave frequencies. By harnessing the unique capabilities of radio and microwave electromagnetic waves and integrating advanced digital holography techniques, this approach promises to enhance imaging resolution and precision in diverse applications, from medical diagnostics to geological surveys and beyond.

3.1 Nature-inspired Multi-sensor Systems for RF Detection and Recognition

Nature offers remarkable examples of advanced sensory systems that can inspire innovative technologies. For instance:

- Spiders: Have four to eight eyes to monitor their web.
- Mosquitoes: Possess hundreds of angularly tilted, spatially distributed sensors.
- Flies: Have two compound eyes, each consisting of hundreds of angularly tilted sensors, providing instant detection, tracking, and recognition of multiple threats in their surroundings (Figure 3.1).

Inspired by these natural systems, particularly the fly's compound eyes, a multi-sensor Fly Eye system has been designed for advanced RF detection and recognition. The Fly Eye system provides an extensive observation area, instantly covering a wide field of view without the need for mechanical scanning. The system is capable of fast, multi-channel signal processing, allowing for the simultaneous detection and tracking of multiple objects or threats. The integration of a new digital holographic technique enhances the system's ability to recognize objects reliably in high-scattering mediums. This technique leverages the properties of coherent diffraction imaging and Fourier transform holography to capture detailed information about objects.

Just as a fly can instantly detect and react to threats, the Fly Eye RF system provides immediate detection and recognition capabilities, crucial for dynamic and fast-changing environments. The digital holographic approach ensures high-resolution imaging by capturing the diffraction patterns of RF waves, allowing for accurate object recognition even in challenging conditions. The system's design allows for scalability, making it adaptable to various applications, from surveillance to biomedical imaging, where rapid and reliable detection is essential.

The nature-inspired Fly Eye RF detection and recognition system represents a significant advancement in sensor technology. By emulating the sophisticated sensory mechanisms of flies, this system offers a powerful tool for high-resolution, rapid, and reliable object recognition in high-scattering

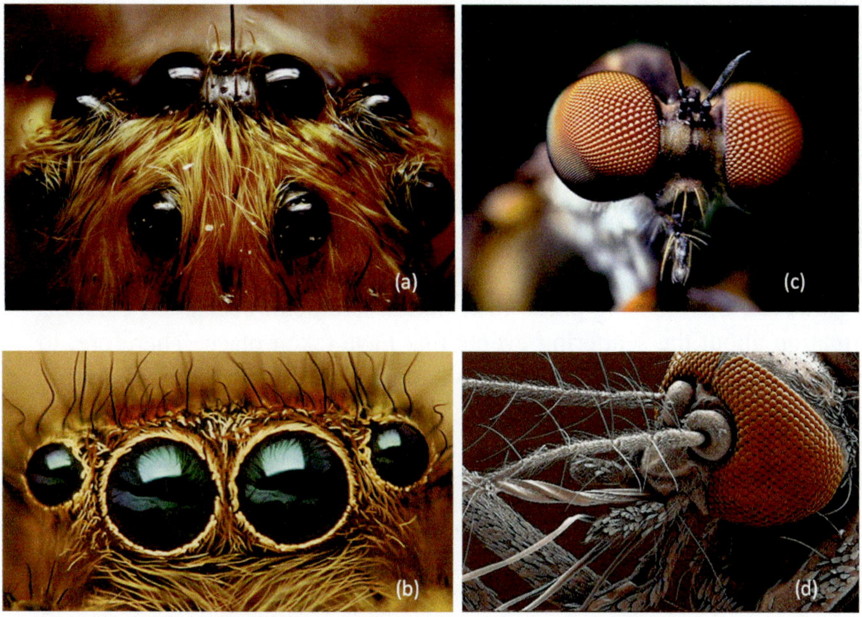

Figure 3.1 Insect vision systems comprising from two to hundreds of sensors for instant threat detection, tracking, and recognition. (a), (b) Thomas B. H. Schroeder, Jared Houghtaling, Bodo D. Wilts, and Michael Mayer, It's Not a Bug, "It's a Feature: Functional Materials in Insects" Advanced materials, Review, www.admat.de, ©2018 The Authors. Published by WILEY-VCH Verlag GmbH & Co. KGaA, Weinheim. Reproduced with permission.355 Copyright 2017, the Royal Society; (c) Lukas Jonaitis, CC-BY-2.0 via Wikimedia Commons; (d) https://oxbow.columbusstate.edu/oxbow-at-home-buggy-bonanza/.

mediums. The integration of digital holography further enhances its capabilities, making it a versatile solution for a wide range of applications.

This chapter outlines the process of object recognition in high-scattering mediums using radio/microwave electromagnetic waves. The process involves several critical steps:

The first step in the process involves digitally recording the diffraction pattern of the object. This step encompasses detecting coherent diffraction components of radio/microwave waves that are reflected/scattered by the entire object and the surrounding medium. These components possess an angular spectrum distribution.

The second step involves recognizing the object based on its spectrum signature. This signature is calculated by performing a Fourier transform and filtering on the recorded distribution pattern.

For accurate object recognition, the recorded distribution pattern should encompass comprehensive information about the waves reflected/scattered by the object and the medium.

The recording distribution pattern comprises three key parts:

Detection of coherent diffraction components. Initially, coherent diffraction components of radio frequency waves reflected by the object and medium are detected. While detectors only capture the intensity, the phase distribution of the wave, which contains vital scattering event information, is lost. However, this missing phase distribution is crucial because it contains information about the scattering events that have taken place. Therefore, to reconstruct the distribution of diffraction components, the phases missing in the detector plane must be recovered. This constitutes the phase problem. Holography solves the phase problem by adding a reference wave with a known distribution to the unknown object wave [1–4].

Solving phase ambiguity. To solve the phase ambiguity, a combination of coherent diffraction imaging (CDI) and digital Fourier transform holography (FTH) techniques is employed. Holography provides a challenging solution to the so-called phase problem. By knowing the phase distribution of the reference wave, it is possible to reconstruct the phase distribution of the object wave, and subsequently, the object distribution from the hologram.

CDI records the diffracted (or scattered) waves in the far field. The diffraction waves distribution of the object can then be reconstructed by calculating the Fourier transform of the recorded hologram. FTH combines the key advantages of two other lensless imaging techniques: the added reference wave solves the phase problem, and the scattered/diffracted waves are recorded, allowing for the acquisition of high-resolution information.

The outlined process of digital recording and object recognition in high-scattering mediums using radio/microwave electromagnetic waves is robust and comprehensive. By integrating CDI and FTH techniques, the process effectively addresses the phase problem and enhances the resolution and accuracy of object recognition. This advanced approach enables the detailed reconstruction of objects even in challenging high-scattering environments.

An important part of the recording of the distribution of diffraction patterns in the high-scattering medium is an angular spectrum of diffracted/scattered waves describing the distribution of scattering of diffraction component vectors. Each diffracting or scattering point of the object creates diffracting wave components, which add to the recording hologram. Radio/microwave long wavelength signals and diffracted components penetrating the human body or underground on a distance of few wavelengths, which corresponds to Fresnel near-field area. The contribution of these wave components can be calculated by adding to the contributions directly reflected by object plane waves and must be taken into account as the change of wave intensity and phase shifts. These diffracting wave components are broadening of the angular spectrum of the disturbance during propagation.

For optical systems wherein the wavelength is a very short relative distance to recording hologram Z. Diffracting wave components are rapidly attenuating by the propagation phenomenon on the distance of a few centimeters, which includes a few hundred or thousands wavelengths and corresponding to far-field area criterium. Such components are called evanescent waves [5, 6].

Scattering of diffraction wave components has good penetration and creates significant contribution to angular spectrum distribution at radio or microwave frequencies. Their wavelength can reach a few tens of centimeters and as a result record holograms of objects at distances up to a few meters, which is smaller than two to three wavelengths and corresponds to the criterium of Fresnel near-field area [7–10].

Proposed object imaging also involves recording digital diffraction patterns, including the suppression of medium-diffracted/scattered components and other noises through the application of reference antennas [11–17].

3.2 Utilizing Radio Frequency Continuous Waves for Object Recognition

Radio frequency (RF) waves offer superior contrast in imaging human tissues compared to X-rays. Their low-power, non-ionizing nature makes them a promising choice for object recognition and biomedical imaging. One key technology that enhances the utility of RF waves in these applications is holography. Holography allows for the recording of both the amplitude and phase distributions of scattered waves within a single holographic record. This recorded data can then be used for numerical reconstruction, enabling the retrieval of object properties such as absorption and phase shifting.

When coherent continuous wave (CW) signals illuminate an object, the resulting far-field reflected signals maintain coherence with uniform frequency and wavelength, as described by the Cittert–Zernike theorem (CZT). However, the absence of near-field diffracted components within these far-field wavefronts prevents accurate reconstruction of the object's shape (Figure 3.2).

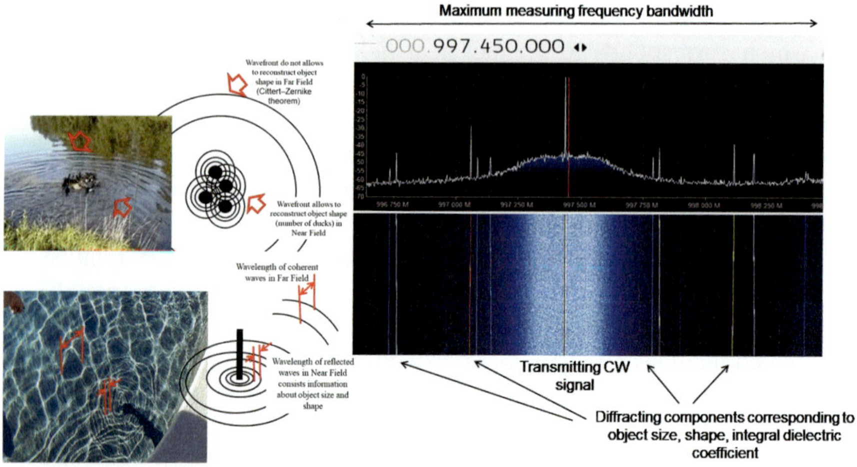

Figure 3.2 The illustration of ducks creating waves on the water surface helps to explain how wavefronts can provide information about the objects that generated them, particularly in the context of near-field and far-field zones. As the waves travel further from the ducks, they become more uniform and coherent, the detailed structure of the wavefronts is lost.

In contrast, wavefronts within the near field contain essential information about reflecting wave objects, including temporal and phase shifts that facilitate precise reconstruction of the object's size and shape. Moreover, the object's dielectric coefficient introduces a phase shift proportional to the continuous wave, similar to the concept of the impedance Smith chart. This additional phase and frequency shift is crucial for object recognition.

By leveraging the detailed information contained within near-field wavefronts, the proposed RF continuous wave imaging system can achieve high-resolution object recognition. This capability is pivotal in applications such as biomedical imaging, where the accurate depiction of internal structures is required without the risks associated with ionizing radiation. The use of holography further enhances the system's ability to capture and reconstruct detailed object properties, making it a powerful tool for non-invasive diagnostics and other advanced imaging applications.

By using the analogy of ducks creating waves on a water surface, Figure 3.2 effectively demonstrates the difference between near-field and far-field wavefronts. This visual aid helps to illustrate why near-field information is crucial for accurate object recognition, as it contains detailed information about the size, shape, and number of objects, whereas far-field wavefronts lose this detail and cannot be used for precise reconstruction. This concept is directly applicable to RF wavefront imaging, where capturing near-field wavefronts is essential for high-resolution object recognition.

3.2.1 Importance of near-field information in RF wavefront imaging

The near-field area for RF wavefront imaging is defined by the field/distance wherein multiple diffracted phase/frequency-shifted components remain detectable and measurable due to the medium's transfer properties. Through careful consideration of the medium's absorption characteristics and resulting wave behavior, this technique presents an innovative and effective approach for achieving high-resolution imaging.

In the near-field zone, detailed wavefronts provide critical information about the object, including its size, shape, and dielectric properties. The reflected signals in the time-space domain are converted into the frequency domain. This transformation allows for the filtering of frequency components that convey essential object details.

Frequency components corresponding to the object's shape, size, and dielectric coefficient can be filtered in the frequency domain. This process creates a unique spectrum signature associated with the object.

The diffraction of continuous waves generates additional frequency components that correspond to the object's size and shape in the near field. These components, unlike harmonics, fall within the range of 5%–20% relative to the transmission frequency.

Capturing and analyzing near-field wavefronts is crucial for high-resolution RF wavefront imaging. This technique, illustrated through the analogy of ducks creating waves, highlights the importance of near-field information for precise object recognition. By converting time-space domain signals into the frequency domain and filtering for specific frequency components, the proposed method provides a unique spectrum signature of the object. This approach enables high-resolution imaging and object recognition, overcoming the limitations imposed by far-field wavefronts and the traditional diffraction limit.

3.3 Detection of Coherent Diffraction Components for Radio Frequency Waves

Coherent diffraction imaging (CDI) is a high-resolution imaging technique that plays a crucial role in the detection of coherent diffraction components for radio frequency (RF) waves. CDI leverages the principles of diffraction to capture detailed information about an object, enabling the reconstruction of high-resolution images. CDI involves recording the diffracted and scattered waves from an object. These waves contain critical information about the object's size, shape, absorption, and dielectric properties. The diffracted waves are captured as a diffraction pattern, which serves as the foundational data for subsequent image reconstruction. By capturing high-order diffraction components, CDI allows for the acquisition of high-resolution data. This is particularly advantageous for imaging small objects or features with fine details.

When the wavelength of the RF waves is considerably larger than the object's size, the resulting diffraction pattern distribution remains invariant to the object's spatial position. This characteristic ensures that the captured data accurately represents the object's properties, regardless of its orientation or location within the imaging field. This capability makes CDI an invaluable tool for high-resolution imaging and precise object recognition in various fields.

3.3.1 Solving phase ambiguity by combination of CDI and digital FTH techniques

Holography emerges as a solution to the phase problem prevalent in coherent imaging. By acquiring the phase distribution of a reference wave, it becomes possible to reconstruct the phase distribution of the object wave and subsequently determine the object distribution from the recorded hologram. In the realm of coherent diffraction imaging (CDI), the waves diffracted (or scattered) by an object are captured in the far field. The distribution of these diffraction waves from the object can be reconstructed by conducting a simple Fourier transform of the recorded hologram (FTH). This approach amalgamates the favorable attributes of two other lensless imaging methods. The addition of a reference wave resolves the phase problem, while the recording of scattered/diffracted waves enables high-resolution data acquisition [1–4].

3.3.2 Significance of scattering vector for recording of diffraction pattern

In accordance with scalar diffraction theory, "the complex field distribution of a monochromatic disturbance can be Fourier-analyzed across any plane, resulting in various spatial Fourier components represented as plane waves traveling in diverse directions away from the given plane. The field amplitude at another point or parallel plane can then be calculated by combining these plane waves while considering the phase shifts endured during propagation" [5].

These spatial components are evaluated through the angular spectrum method. In this approach, for a system of monochromatic sources $A = \pi r^2$, a wave is incident on a transverse (x, y) plane traveling with a component of propagation in the positive z direction. The complex field across the field U(x, y, z) that appears across a recording antennas plane at distance z from object can be given as an inverse Fourier transform of its spectrum [1, 5, 6]:

$$U\,(x, y, 0) = \iint_{-\infty}^{\infty} A\,(f_x, f_y; 0)\,\exp[j2\pi(f_x x + f_y y)]df_x df_y. \qquad (3.1)$$

Thus across the plane $z = 0$, a complex-exponential function exp $[j2\pi(f_x x + f_y y)]$ may be regarded as representing a plane wave propagating with direction cosines (Figure 3.3)

$$\alpha = \lambda f_x, \quad \beta = \lambda f_y, \quad \gamma = \sqrt[2]{1 - (\lambda f_x)^2 - (\lambda f_y)^2}. \qquad (3.2)$$

The inverse Fourier transform of *U*, the complex amplitude of the plane-wave component with spatial frequencies (f_x, f_y) is simply $A(f_x, f_y; 0)df_x df_y$, evaluated at $(f_x = \alpha/\lambda,\ f_y = \beta/\lambda)$. For this reason, the function is called the angular spectrum of the disturbance *U*(*x*,*y*,0) and can be presented as:

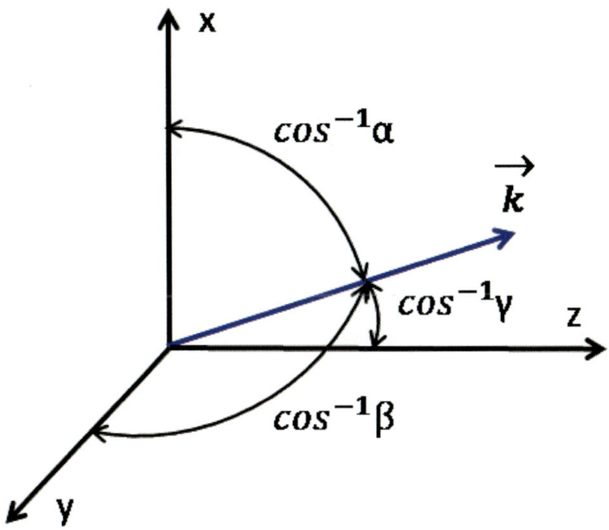

Figure 3.3 Visualization of the wave vector.

$$A\left(\frac{\alpha}{\lambda},\frac{\beta}{\lambda},0\right)=\iint_{-\infty}^{\infty}U(x,y;0)\exp\left[-j2\pi\left(\frac{\alpha}{\lambda}\mathrm{x}+\frac{\beta}{\lambda}y\right)\right]dxdy. \quad (3.3)$$

Importantly, the angular spectrum is broadened by the object's diffraction, with the extent of broadening contingent on the object's size relative to the wavelength. In optical systems, where wavelengths range from approximately 380 to 750 nanometers, these spatial wave components are rapidly attenuated due to propagation. These components, referred to as evanescent waves, experience rapid attenuation over a short distance of a few centimeters, where one centimeter encompasses a few hundred wavelengths.

In the context of radio/microwave frequencies, the wavelength of diffracted components can extend to several tens of centimeters. Consequently, attenuation of these longer wavelength components within the human body or underground over a distance of a few wavelengths (equivalent to one to two meters) is minimal. The contribution of these diffracted components over such distances substantially influences the amplitude and phase distribution in the digital hologram, thereby significantly impacting image resolution and the diffraction component spectrum. Additionally, this approach allows for the recording of holograms of objects up to a few meters away, aligning with the criteria of the Fresnel near-field area.

In scenarios where coherent continuous waves illuminate an object, the resulting reflected diffracting components in the far field exhibit coherency, featuring uniform frequency and wavelength. However, due to the absence of near-field diffracted components, these far-field wavefronts do not lend themselves to accurate shape reconstruction. Conversely, wavefronts within the near field encapsulate invaluable information concerning reflected waves, encompassing temporal and phase shifts that enable precise object shape reconstruction. Furthermore, the object's dielectric coefficient introduces a proportional phase shift for continuous waves. This additional phase shift provides additional information crucial for image resolution and recognition of the object.

3.4 Recording Angular Spectrum with Wide Beam Sensors Covering Whole Object

The combination of coherent diffraction imaging (CDI) and digital Fourier transform holography (FTH) techniques is commonly applied in far-field areas where rapidly attenuated diffracted/scattered components (evanescent waves) are disregarded [2, 7–10]. For Fresnel coherent diffraction imaging

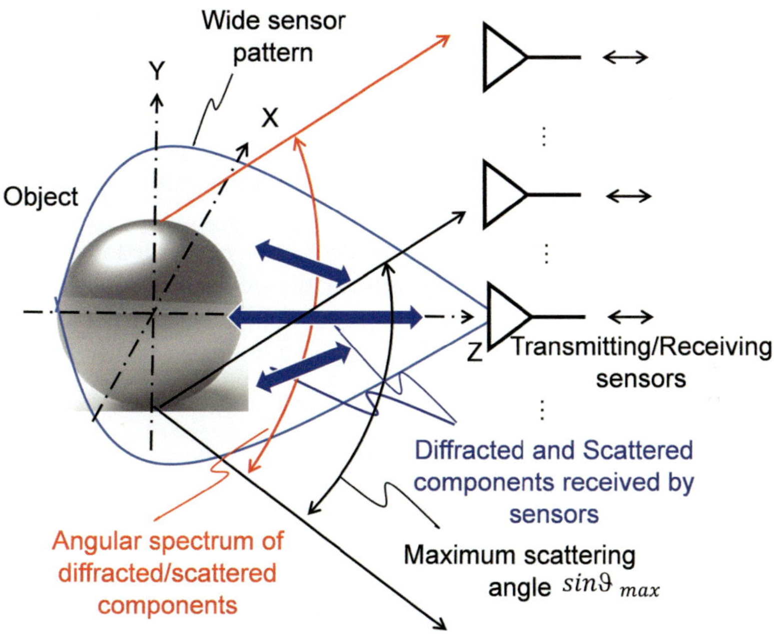

Figure 3.4 Diagram illustrating the recording of diffracted and scattered components within the Fresnel near-field region using a sensor array with wide sensor patterns.

(FCDI), it becomes imperative to incorporate the recording of the angular spectrum. Figure 3.4 illustrates a diagram showcasing the recording of diffracted/scattered components within the Fresnel near-field region using an antenna array with multiple transmitting and receiving sensors equipped with wide sensor patterns. These patterns ensure the receipt of the angular spectrum of the diffracted/scattered components across the entire maximum scattering angle. The angular spectrum captures alterations in wave intensity and phase shifts, which are detected by the array of antennas.

3.5 Recording Diffraction Patterns with Digital Holographic System

The concept of holography corresponding to Encyclopedia Britannica describing: "Every part of a hologram contains the image of the whole object. You can cut off the corner of a hologram and see the entire image through it. For every viewing angle you see the image in a different perspective, as you would a real object. Each piece of a hologram contains a particular perspective of the image, but it includes the entire object."

The proposed technology utilizes hologram recording through an array of staring sensors with wide numerical apertures, as depicted in Figure 3.5. Each staring sensor is endowed with a wide numerical aperture, enabling it to cover the entire object or an illuminated section. Consequently, it captures reflected/scattered segments of the object's illuminating beam. In this configuration, every small segment of the digitally recorded hologram, or holographic matrix, contains partial information about the entire object. The entirety of the hologram matrix encompasses comprehensive data for the reconstruction of a 3D image of the object or the illuminated part of it. This

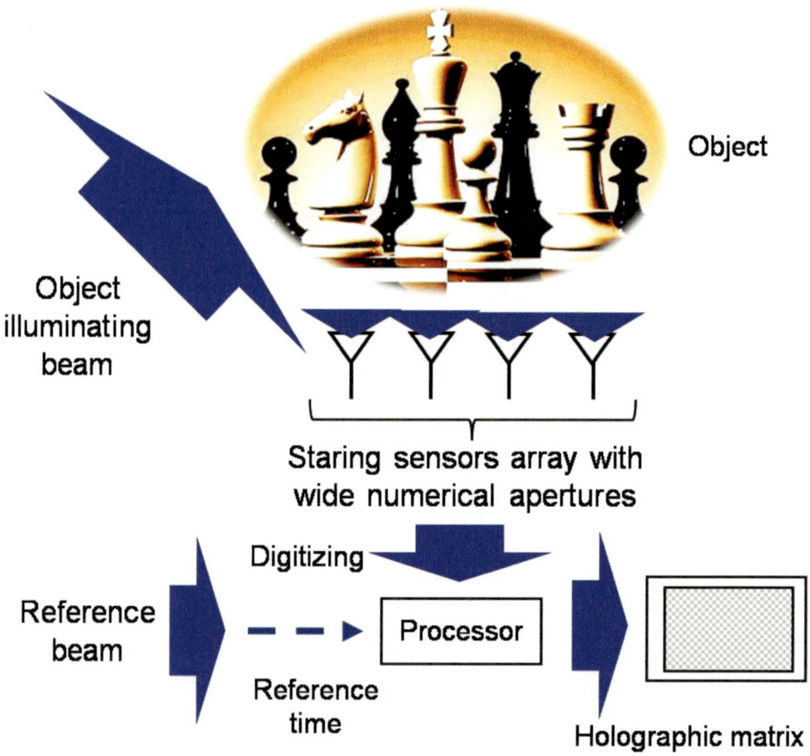

Figure 3.5 An array of staring sensors with wide numerical apertures need to be used for recording of a holographic matrix consisting of information about scattered, diffracted, and angular distribution of diffraction pattern components.

intrinsic difference between the recording of a regular image and a hologram stands out as a crucial aspect of the technology.

The wide numerical aperture of each sensor plays a pivotal role in recording information about the entire object in each segment of the hologram or digitally in the holographic matrix. Moreover, sensors simultaneously covering the object from different directions contribute additional 3D information about the size, shape, and dielectric properties for the viewpoint of an object or multiple objects. Consequently, the recorded holographic matrix contains supplementary information about the object, facilitating the reconstruction of the object's image with significantly enhanced resolution and more reliable recognition. This holographic matrix can be effectively applied for the reconstruction of a three-dimensional image (Figure 3.6).

The system for recording diffraction patterns as a digital hologram is presented in Figure 3.7. Each sensor with a wide numerical aperture needs

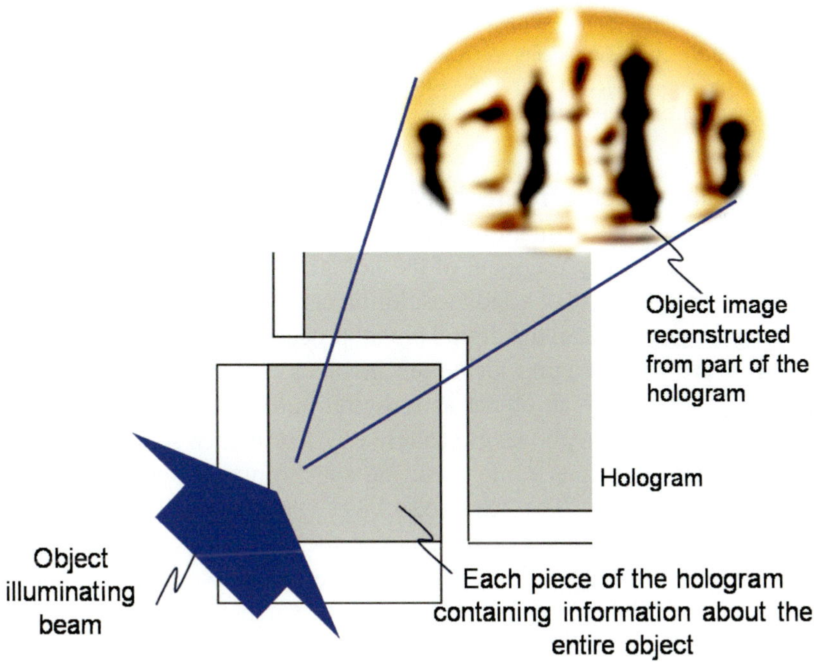

Figure 3.6 Array of sensors with wide numerical aperture covering the entire object allows recording of the hologram, wherein each sensor pattern contains information represents a viewpoint of the entire object.

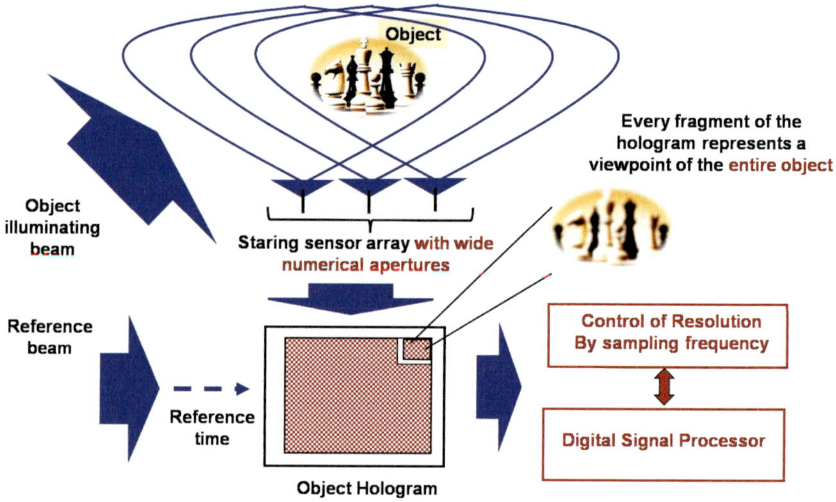

Figure 3.7 Every sensor with a wide numerical aperture needs to cover entire object. Reference beam providing reference time for recording phase shifts and angular distribution of scattered and diffracted components. As result, every fragment of the hologram represents a viewpoint of the entire object. Control of vision resolution can be provided by control of sampling frequency from digital signal processor.

to cover the entire object. A reference beam provides the reference time for recording phases and the angular distribution of scattered and diffracted components. As a result, every fragment of the hologram represents a viewpoint of the entire object. Control of vision resolution can be achieved by adjusting the sampling frequency from the digital signal processor.

The RF wavefront imaging technique involves the real-time recording of RF waves scattered by an object as a digital hologram. These scattered waves are superimposed with waves scattered by a reference source situated in the same processing time frame, ensuring synchronization via processor time or sampling circuits. The scattered object waves are collected by an array of overlapping antennas, which cover the entire observation area, including the object. Meanwhile, the scattered reference waves are directly received from an RF signal source and/or reference antennas. By employing signals from these overlapping antennas and reference antennas as sources for scattered/reference signals, the reconstruction process becomes simplified, yielding enhanced image resolution.

RF wavefront imaging constitutes a lensless imaging technique, wherein RF waves scattered by an object interact with waves scattered by a reference

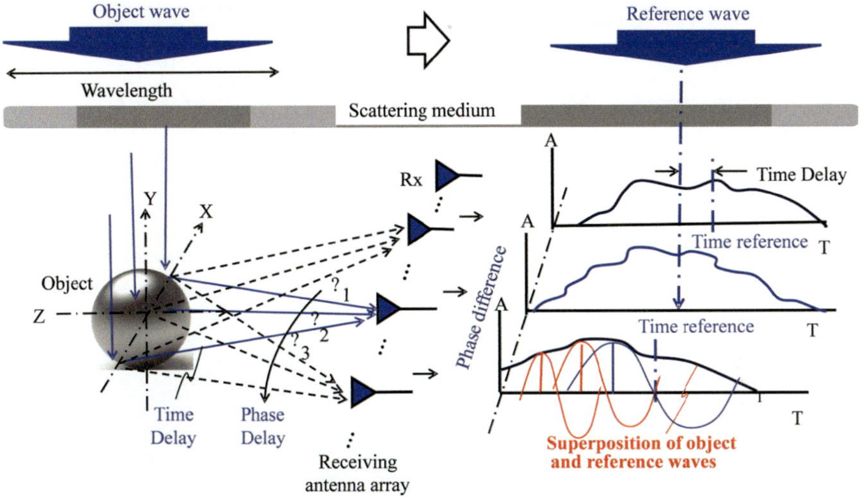

Figure 3.8 Detection of RF diffracting components through an array of antennas with overlapping antenna patterns for the recording of a digital hologram. The superposition of diffraction components received by multiple antennas simultaneously covers the entire object recording, with a temporal reference to the reference wave.

source within the same processing time frame or plane, as illustrated in Figure 3.8.

RF waves undergo diffraction on the object's surface, and the resulting diffracted components are concurrently received by an array of sensors positioned at a distance Z from the object. This sensor array can be distributed in a 2D plane along the X and Y axes or on a spherical surface, with dimensions large enough to capture all of the object's diffracted components, limited by the maximum scattering angle (θ_{max}). Each sensor receives diffracted components with distinct time and phase delays, corresponding to the distance between the object's scattering point and the sensor along the X or Y axis. This process holds for both axes. Each sensor must receive diffracted components reflected from all scattering points of the entire object, thus forming the basis for reconstructing a high-resolution 3D image of the object.

The technique involves the superposition of RF wave components diffracted by an object and those received by multiple sensors with corresponding time frames or planes. This is achieved using the time reference of the reference wave or synchronizing circuits within the processor or sampling system. The recording of diffraction components as a digital hologram,

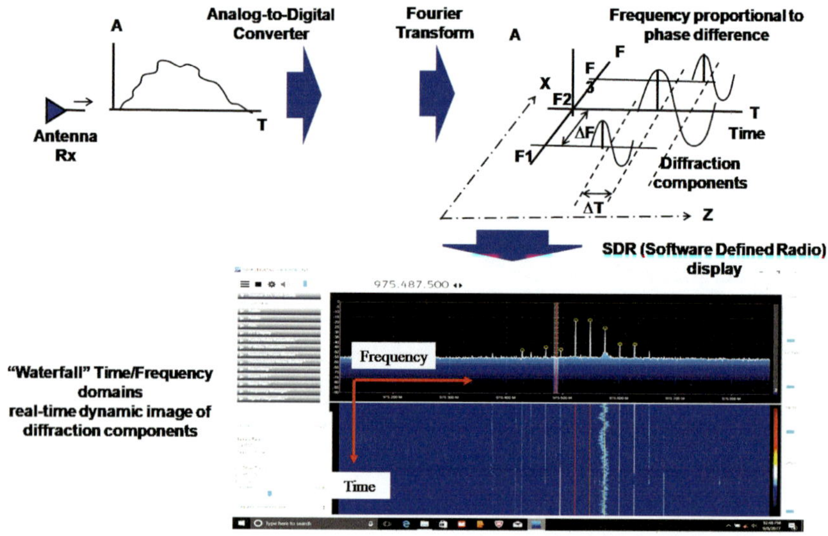

Figure 3.9 Recording of diffraction components representing the part of digital hologram receiving by one sensor.

representing part of the whole object digital hologram, is presented in the diagram in Figure 3.9. RF waves cover the entire object simultaneously, and scattered waves from multiple points are received by each antenna with different phase and time delays. These diffraction components are superimposed in each detector, forming part of a hologram received by one antenna. After digitizing and applying a Fourier transform, the diffracting components can be observed as time-frequency domains in a real-time dynamic image, often referred to as a "waterfall."

Digital information from all sensors forms a raw data matrix in the processor. Superimposing diffraction components received by separate antennas, corresponding within the same time frame but with time shifts along the X, Y, and Z axes, allows for the formation of a digital hologram representing the whole object with a 3D view of the part covered by the sensor array. In Figure 3.10, two samples of possible distribution of wide numerical aperture sensors around imaging object are presented.

This comprehensive digital hologram encompasses detailed spatial information about the object, enabling high-resolution three-dimensional imaging and accurate object recognition [11, 12].

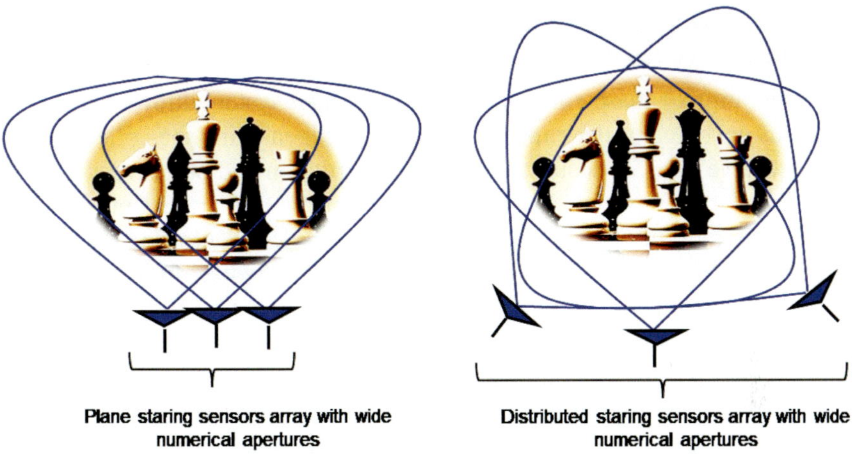

Figure 3.10 Distribution of staring sensors to recording digital hologram.

3.6 Test Setup

As previously discussed, object recognition by the spectrum signature is calculated through the Fourier transform and filtering of the recorded distribution pattern. The digital recording of an object's distribution pattern includes the detection of coherent diffraction components of radio/microwave frequency waves reflected/scattered by the entire object and the surrounding medium, capturing the angular spectrum distribution.

The test setup for this process involves the following components:

1. Transceiver antenna module (TAM): This module is responsible for transmitting electromagnetic signals and receiving the scattered and diffracted patterns. It ensures that the signals captured contain the maximum possible information about the objects and the scattering medium.
2. Multi-channel monopulse signal processor (MSP): This processor provides direct detection, digitizing, and monopulse signal processing. It processes the received signals to extract range and positioning information.
3. Holographic database (HOB): This component handles the real-time recording of data, calculates object parameters, and generates images. It maintains a holographic database that serves as a centralized repository

for structured and semi-structured data, facilitating data visualization and intelligence reporting.

The integration of these components into a unified system allows for the simultaneous coverage of the entire observation area, enabling the collection of comprehensive data for accurate image reconstruction and object recognition. The setup must ensure that every fragment of the hologram represents a viewpoint of the entire object, with vision resolution controlled by the sampling frequency of the digital signal processor. Unified setup for object recognition by spectrum signature is presented in Figure 3.11.

The transceiver antenna module encompasses an antenna array, where each antenna is linked to a signal conditioning circuit and a software defined radio (SDR). This configuration permits the reception of RF signals from the object area with suitable signal conditioning. The monopulse signal processor serves as a pivotal component, featuring a multi-channel monopulse processor and synchronization means. This processing unit is tasked with handling received RF signals. Digitized holographic data forming real-time digital hologram and performing necessary signal processing and analysis to generate meaningful images and recognize objects [14–17].

The setup also comprises vision control means and artificial fabric. Vision control provides control of range, focus, field of view, and direction. Artificial fabric will provide additional means for enhancing imaging and object recognition. These functions will be considered in Chapters 4–6.

Figure 3.12 presents a setup for object recognition in high-scattering mediums. This block diagram outlines an embodiment of an RF-enhanced imaging and recognition system comprising separate transmitting antenna module and receiving antenna modules. The transmitting antenna module comprises a separate signal generator with a transmitting antenna. Receiving antenna module comprises additional reference antenna. This system is designed to facilitate advanced RF-based imaging and object recognition at radio/microwave frequencies.

The separate signal generator, together with its associated transmitting antenna, generates and emits RF signals. These signals interact with the object area, and their reflections are captured by the antenna array within the receiving module. To enhance imaging accuracy by mitigating unwanted signal interferences, a separate reference antenna is introduced into the system. The connection by digital interface between the receiver antenna module, monopulse signal processor, and holographic database including an imaging

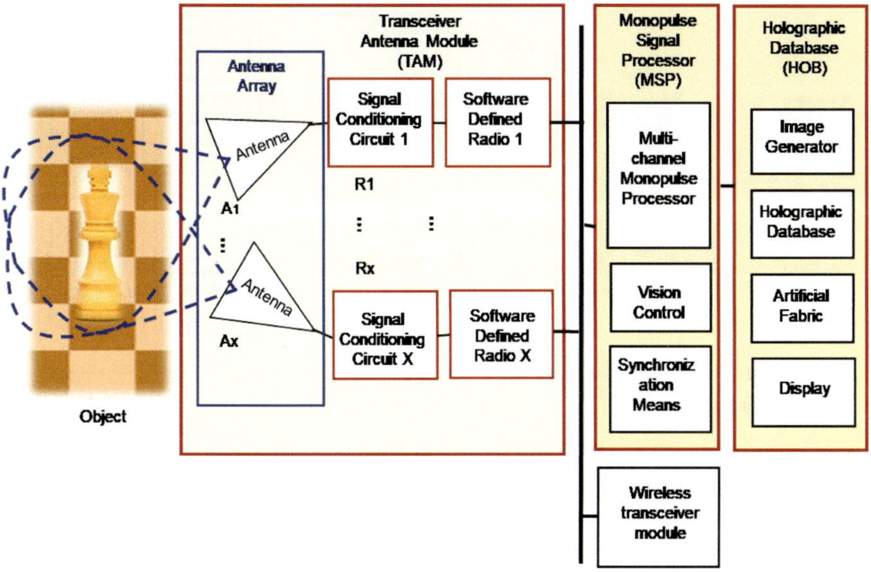

Figure 3.11 Unified setup for imaging and recognition of objects by spectrum signatures.

generator and display enables the processed data to be translated into visual images for easy interpretation and analysis.

Monopulse processing, incorporated within the system, enhances accuracy in direction finding and phase delay measurement, contributing to improved imaging resolution [13]. When recording digital holograms for RF diffraction imaging, one or more antenna arrays must concurrently cover the entire object or observation area.

Traditional scanning systems with narrow beams might not capture all scattered and diffracted signals, particularly those reflected outside the antenna's field of view. To address this, multiple antenna arrays can be positioned along multiple axes to ensure comprehensive coverage and the recording of a digital hologram. A planar antenna array is particularly suitable for capturing RF diffraction imaging holograms of wide observation areas. By positioning these planar antenna arrays strategically, it is possible to achieve a more detailed and comprehensive recording of the diffracted and scattered signals from the object. This setup ensures that all pertinent signals are captured, enabling the construction of high-resolution digital holograms that provide accurate three-dimensional representations of the observed objects.

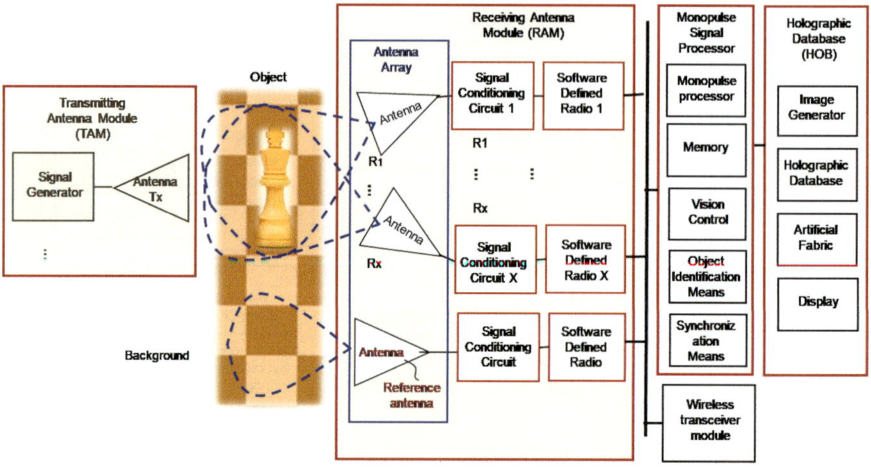

Figure 3.12 Block diagram of an embodiment of an RF-enhanced imaging and recognition system in high-scattered mediums.

3.7 Recognition of Different Materials by Spectrum Signature

Various kinds of materials and objects, including metal, dielectric, organic, and liquid, have been tested for recognition using continuous wave signals with a wavelength of approximately one foot, corresponding to a frequency

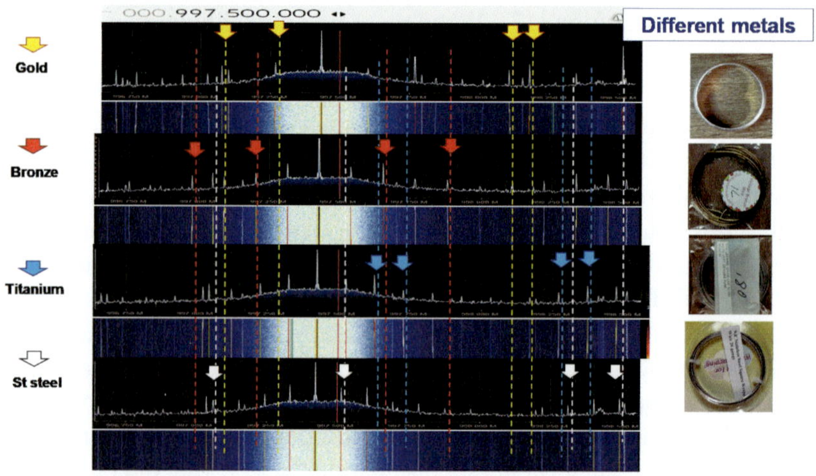

Figure 3.13 Recognition of different metals, bronze, titanium, and steel by spectrum signature.

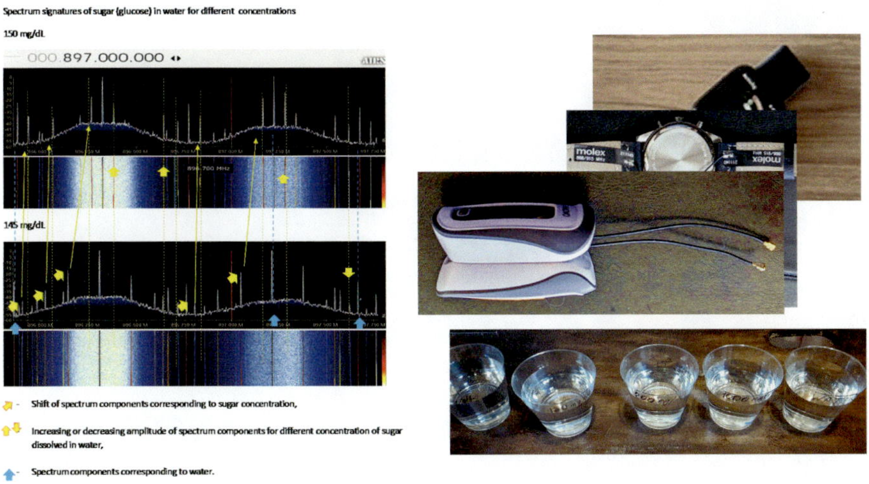

Figure 3.18 Measurement of glucose concentration in water by spectrum signature.

Figure 3.19 Underground detection of plastic bucket with fertilizer, and detection of a plastic bag with fertilizer hidden inside laptop. Two handheld detector models and directional antennas were applied for the test.

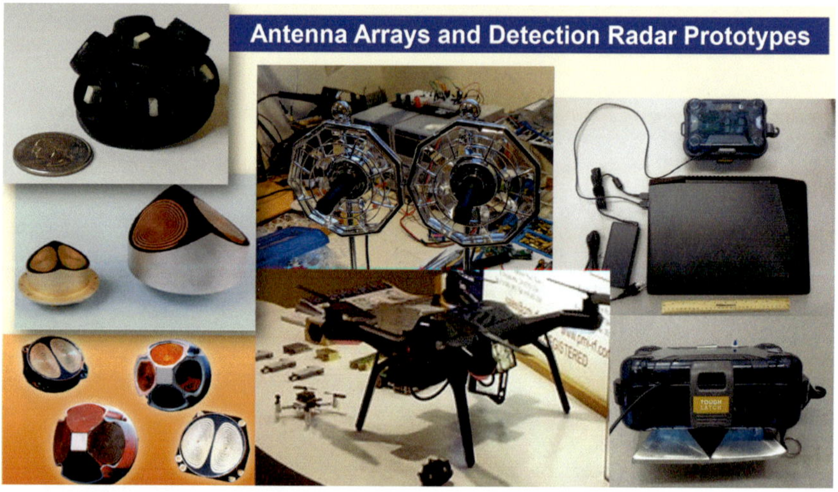

Figure 3.20 Directional antenna arrays, small and nano-drones with installed detection systems and handheld detector model applied for test.

Figure 3.21 Working models of handheld radio/microwave systems applied for remote recognition of different materials.

By analyzing these spectrum signatures, it is possible to distinguish between different types of materials. Each material exhibits a distinct pattern in the frequency domain, which can be used as a fingerprint for identification.

The ability to filter and recognize these unique signatures enables the system to accurately identify and classify various objects and materials based on their spectral characteristics.

In Figures 3.20–3.21, antenna arrays with directional antennas and radar models used for measurement system parameters and for recognition experiments are presented.

The modification of working models of handheld radio/microwave systems applied for remote recognition of different materials is presented in Figure 3.21. Imaging and recognition systems can be very small and positioned on drones for remote object identification.

Conclusion

Radio and microwave electromagnetic waves offer significant advantages due to their ability to penetrate diverse materials such as human tissues, walls, and the ground. The low-power RF signals pose minimal risk of ionizing damage to humans, making them an excellent choice for imaging applications across various domains. The primary challenge in achieving high-resolution imaging and object recognition within human bodies or underground environments lies in the high-scattering of signals inside objects and mediums.

The proposed technique for object recognition in high-scattering mediums, particularly human bodies or underground settings, focuses on incorporating the angular spectrum of diffracted/scattered components for Fresnel (near-field) recording of digital object distribution patterns. The inherent limitations of image resolution, often constrained by the minimum pixel size, can be overcome by utilizing digital holograms. In this method, the minimum resolution is determined by the minimum digital sampling and/or phase measurement step, remaining invariant to the relatively long wavelengths of radio and microwave frequencies.

By performing a Fourier transform and filtering the distribution of diffracting components from reference antennas, the technique enables the separation of objects from the surrounding medium based on their spectrum signatures. This approach captures diffraction components that contain vital information about an object's dielectric properties, size, and shape, all of which remain unaffected by its spatial position.

Additional information about the object is gleaned by processing the digital hologram signals across the frequency, time, and spatial domains. The spatial domain represents the object's position in space measured by the directions of signal arrival, which are then transformed into phase/time delay. The strategic placement of receiving antennas along multiple axes provides additional multi-axis information about the object, thereby enhancing imaging resolution.

References

[1] T. Latychevskaia, H. Fink, "Practical algorithms for simulation and reconstruction of digital in-line holograms," Physics Department, University of Zurich, Winterthurerstrasse 190, 8057 Zurich, Switzerland, [Online] Available tatiana@physik.uzh.ch [Accessed April 10, 2023].

[2] T. Latychevskaia, J. Longchamp, and H. Fink "When holography meets coherent diffraction imaging," Institute of Physics, University of Zurich, Winterthurerstrasse 190, CH-8057, Switzerland * [Online] Available tatiana@physik.uzh.ch [Accessed April 10, 2023].

[3] T. Latychevskaia, A. Kohli "Low-dose shift- and rotation-invariant diffraction recognition imaging," Scientific Reports | (2022) 12:11202, [Online] Available https://doi.org/10.1038/s41598-022-15486-y [Accessed April 10, 2023].

[4] S. Mustafi, T. Latychevskaia, "Fourier Transform Holography: A Lensless Imaging Technique," Photonics 2023, 10, 153. [Online] Available https://doi.org/10.3390/photonics10020153, [Accessed April 10, 2023].

[5] J. Ratcliffe, "Some aspects of diffraction theory and their application to the ionosphere," Reports on progress in physics 19, 188 – 267, 1965.

[6] J. Goodman, "Introduction to Fourier optics", 3 ed. Roberts & Company Publishers, 2004.

[7] G. Williams, H. Quiney, B. Dhal, C. Tran, K. Nugent, A. Peele, D. Paterson, and M. de Jonge, "Fresnel coherent diffractive imaging," Phys. Rev. Lett. 97(2), 025506, 2006.

[8] G. Williams, H. Quiney, B. Dahl, C. Tran, A. Peele, K. Nugent, M. De Jonge, and D. Paterson, "Curved beam coherent diffractive imaging," Thin Solid Films 515(14), 5553–5556, 2007.

[9] L. Whitehead, G. Williams, H. Quiney, K. Nugent, D. Paterson, M. de Jonge, and I. McNulty, "Fresnel diffractive imaging: Experimental study of coherence and curvature," Phys. Rev. B 77(10), 104112, 2008.

[10] G. Williams, H. Quiney, A. Peele, and K. Nugent, "Fresnel coherent diffractive imaging: treatment and analysis of data," New J. Phys. 12(3), 035020, 2010.

[11] S. Harman "A comparison of staring radars with scanning radars for UAV detection: introduction of the Alarm ^{TM} staring radar," European Radar Conference (EURAD), EUMA, Sep. 2015.
[12] S. Harman, "Holographic Radar Development," Aveillant Ltd., Cambridge, U.K. 2021-02-07. [Online] Available www.microwavejournal.com [Accessed May 8, 2022].
[13] S. Lipsky, "Microwave Passive Direction Finder," SciTech Publishing Inc. Raleigh, NC 27613, 2004.
[14] P. Molchanov, A. Gorwara, "Fly Eye Radar Concept," IRS2017. International Radar Symposium, Prague, July 2017.
[15] P. Molchanov "Radar for detection of concealed objects," US patent appl. 18/100,882, 01/24/2023.
[16] P. Molchanov, "Multi-beam multi-band antenna array module," US patent application US20240170855A1, November 20, 2022.
[17] P. Molchanov, "Objects Recognition in High-scattering Conditions at Radio/Microwave Frequency," SPIE Defense + Commercial Sensing conference, National Harbor, Washington DC, April, 2024.

4

Human-like Lensless Vision Concept

Introduction

Digital holographic data combined with the Fresnel coherent diffraction imaging (FCDI) analytics tool, as presented in previous chapters, introduces a new RF technology that can offer scalable vision resolution and reliable remote objects/materials recognition by spectrum signature. The chapter below will explore a novel technique that provides human-like capabilities for electronically scalable control of vision focus, field of view (FOV), direction, resolution, and recognition without the need for precise lenses and moving mechanical parts. This revolutionary human-like vision technology enables electronic control of resolution, FOV, focus, and direction. This innovation not only eliminates the need for precision optical systems but also addresses big data challenges associated with transferring vision information for computer vision systems.

The proposed RF vision technology includes the ability to adjust vision resolution electronically that allows for fine-tuning of image clarity and detail without relying on mechanical adjustments. The ability to electronically adjust the FOV allows for dynamic changes in the viewing area, optimizing the vision system for different tasks and requirements. Electronic control over focus and direction enhances the flexibility and functionality of the vision system, making it adaptable to various environments and conditions. Utilizing spectrum signatures, this technology enables the identification and differentiation of various objects and materials from a distance with high reliability.

By moving away from traditional precision optical systems, this technology reduces complexity, cost, and the need for maintenance, while increasing robustness and versatility. The integration of digital holography and FCDI analytics facilitates the efficient handling and processing of large volumes of vision data, improving the performance of computer vision systems.

This novel technology marks a significant advancement in the field of vision systems, offering a versatile and powerful tool for various applications, including biomedical imaging, security, surveillance, and industrial automation. By harnessing the capabilities of RF technology and digital holography, it paves the way for the next generation of high-resolution, adaptive vision systems.

4.1 Human Visual Systems

As mentioned in Chapter 2, we divided the resolution term into two different determinations: the *vision resolution* which represents the resolution between two points or smallest objects, which can provide a remote detection system based on the application of electromagnetic waves (EW), and the *imaging resolution* which represents the level of displayed image details. It will depend on the kind of image display: spatial or digital, and display material or physical properties.

Human visual systems provide three different fields of view (FOV): normal, wide, and precise, as illustrated in Figure 4.1 (a). They also offer controllable focus distance, as shown in Figure 4.1 (b), control of direction (Figure 4.2), and vision resolution.

In the human eye, light enters through the cornea and is focused by the lens onto the retina, a light-sensitive membrane at the back of the eye. The retina serves as a transducer, converting light into neuronal discrete signals. This transduction is achieved by photoreceptive cells of the retina, known as rods and cones, which detect photons of light and respond by producing

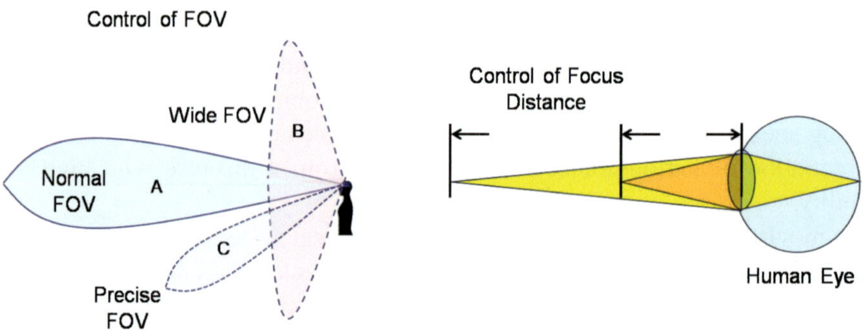

(a) (b)

Figure 4.1 Human visual system can control FOV (a) and focus distance (b).

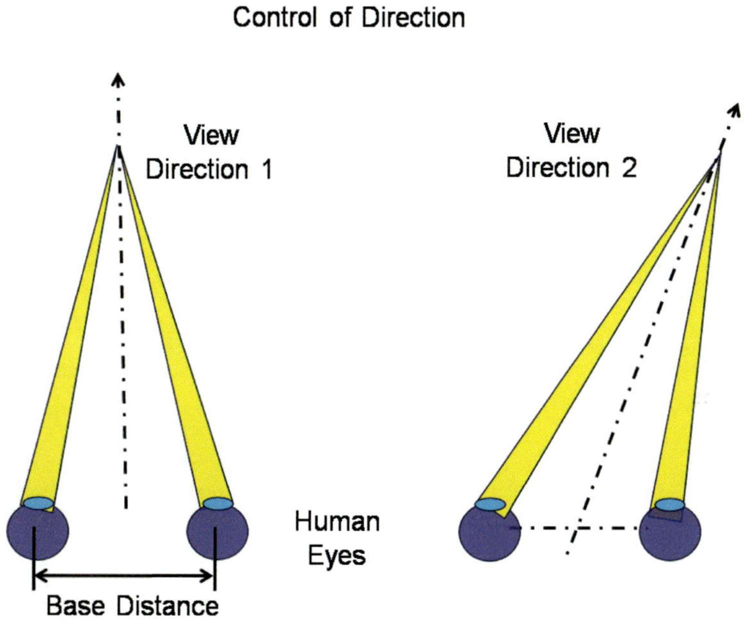

Figure 4.2 Base distance between human eyes provides for human the possibility to control the direction of vision and estimate distance to objects.

neural impulses. These neural signals are transmitted by the optic nerve from the retina upstream to the central ganglia in the brain [Wikipedia]. Remote visual optical systems can mimic some or all of these functions, but they typically rely on precise, expensive optics that are sensitive to illuminating light intensity, as well as adverse weather conditions such as snow, rain, and smog.

Normally maximum human field of vision (visual field) is approximately 190 degrees horizontally and 130 degrees vertically, wherein the human field of vision is the total area in which objects can be seen when the eyes are fixed in one position. However, it's important to note that the quality of vision is not uniform across the entire visual field (Figure 4.3) [1].

The central area of the visual field (fovea), is providing high-acuity vision and color perception. This region has a higher density of cone cells, which are responsible for detailed vision. The peripheral vision, on the other hand, is more sensitive to motion and changes in light levels but has lower acuity. The human vision system is complex and allows perception of a wide range of

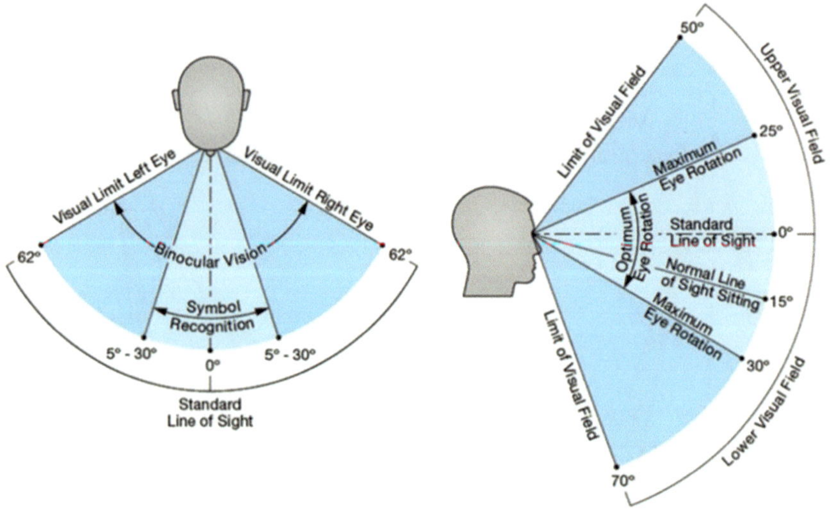

Figure 4.3 Human vision fields by azimuth and elevation.

visual information about surrounding area and enabling humans to navigate and interact with the world.

4.2 Human-like Vision Control in RF Imaging Systems

The main advantages of the application of RF-based vision systems are:

- Weather resilience: Unlike optical systems, RF-based systems are less affected by adverse weather conditions such as fog, rain, and snow, ensuring reliable performance in diverse environments.
- Cost-effectiveness: Eliminating the need for high-precision optics reduces overall system costs.
- Adaptability: Electronic control allows for dynamic adjustments in FOV, focus, direction, and resolution, providing versatility for various applications.
- Enhanced imaging: By processing digital holographic data with FCDI analytics, RF-based systems can achieve high-resolution imaging and accurate object recognition, even in high-scattering mediums.

4.2.1 Controlled vision resolution

The RF remote detection system for limitless vision resolution is described earlier in Chapter 2. The vision resolution of the presented holographic system is determined by the sampling step of the digitizing system. Reflected signals from the object contain information about its shape, size, and dielectric properties.

Sensors with wide numerical apertures receive signals reflected from an entire object (or multiple objects). The superposition of these signals relative to a reference time allows the formation of a hologram. Each fragment of the hologram comprises a viewpoint of the whole object. Fourier transform is the transformation of received signals from the time domain to the frequency domain. It enables electronic control and filtering of the ranges and limits of all frequency components, which contain information about the object and the system's vision parameters. Digitizing these signals allows the system to shift from traditional geometric spatial imaging resolution limits to theoretically limitless scalable resolution. This scalability is determined by the digitizing sampling frequency steps (Figure 4.4).

Figure 4.4 illustrates the concept of digitizing holographic signals, showing the transition from spatial resolution limits to scalable resolution determined by sampling frequency steps. This figure exemplifies how the resolution can be electronically controlled and optimized for different applications.

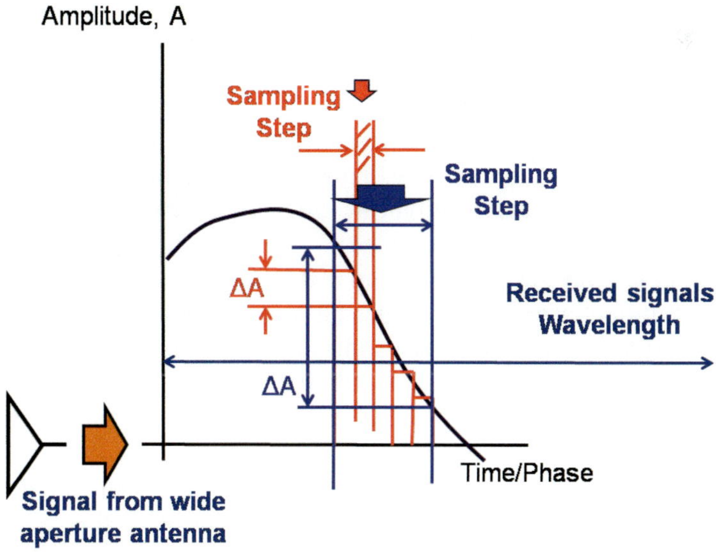

Figure 4.4 Control of sampling step determined by sampling frequency provides the possibility to record real-time digital hologram matrix of objects with different resolutions.

By leveraging the advanced capabilities of RF remote detection and digital holography, the system achieves a level of vision resolution that surpasses traditional optical methods, providing a robust and versatile solution for high-resolution imaging and object recognition.

The resolution of the received digital hologram, or holographic data matrix, will now be limited by the sampling frequency and the stability of both transmitting and sampling frequencies. It's crucial to note that the conditioning front-end circuits coupled to every wide numerical aperture sensor must be fast enough to handle the possible scattered and diffracted frequency components without introducing limitations.

The resolution now is fundamentally determined by the sampling frequency and the stability of both the transmitting and sampling frequencies. This precision ensures that the high-frequency components of the diffracted signals are accurately captured. Front-end circuits must be capable of operating at high speeds to avoid bottlenecking the system. These circuits need to be designed to handle the wide range of frequencies encountered in scattered and diffracted signals. The sampling step, determined by the sampling frequency, allows for the recording of real-time digital hologram matrices of objects at varying resolutions. This flexibility is key to adapting the resolution based on the specific needs of the observation.

Using a wide field of view (FOV), low-resolution imaging enables fast observation of large areas, mimicking human-like vision. This approach minimizes the volume of digital data matrices, making it feasible to transmit data even with limited digital transfer speeds.

For objects requiring more detailed observation, high-resolution imaging can be applied within a narrower FOV. This selective resolution approach ensures that detailed visual information can still be transferred quickly, even when digital transfer speeds are constrained.

Recording of real-time digital hologram matrix provides the capability to switch between different resolution modes allowing for efficient data management. Wide-area, low-resolution scanning can identify regions or objects of interest, which can then be targeted for high-resolution, narrow-FOV imaging. This method balances the need for comprehensive coverage with the ability to focus on details as needed.

By adjusting the resolution and FOV dynamically, the system can manage efficient data transfer. Data volumes effectively, ensuring that critical information is captured and transmitted efficiently without overwhelming the data transfer channels. The system also provides the ability to scale vision resolution electronically, without relying on precise optical components, providing a significant advantage in flexibility and robustness. It allows for real-time adjustments to the resolution based on the immediate needs of the observation, providing both broad overviews and detailed inspections as required.

Emulating human-like vision capabilities, the system can quickly scan large areas at low resolution and then focus on specific points of interest with high resolution. This mimics how the human eye prioritizes and processes visual information, enhancing the system's usability and efficiency. By integrating these aspects, the system not only improves imaging resolution but also enhances its adaptability to various operational scenarios, ensuring efficient data management and robust performance in diverse environments.

4.2.2 Controllable field of view

Human vision has the remarkable ability to control the field of view (FOV), adjusting from normal to narrow or wide. In remote detection and imaging systems, sensors with a wide numerical aperture can similarly offer controllable FOV by managing the range of phase/time delay in the holographic receiving system, as illustrated in Figure 4.5(a,b).

Wide numerical aperture sensors capture a broad spectrum of reflected and scattered signals, enabling a comprehensive FOV. By adjusting the range of phase/time delays that the system measures, the FOV can be controlled dynamically. The field of view in a remote detection and imaging holographic system is governed by restricting the range within which phase delays are measured. This approach allows the system to focus on a specific segment of the captured signals, effectively narrowing or widening the FOV.

The system can fine-tune its overall FOV by adjusting the FOV of each sensor individually. This can be achieved through specialized algorithms that modulate the phase delay range. Controlling the number of sensors activated along specific axes further refines the FOV. This method enables the system to adapt its FOV based on the number of active sensors and their spatial configuration.

Specialized digital coding programs are utilized to process the holographic data matrix, implementing FOV adjustments. These programs can dynamically manage the FOV, providing tailored imaging capabilities for different operational scenarios.

The ability to control the FOV allows for greater flexibility in imaging. This adaptability is crucial for applications requiring both broad area scans and focused, high-resolution inspections. By controlling the FOV, the system

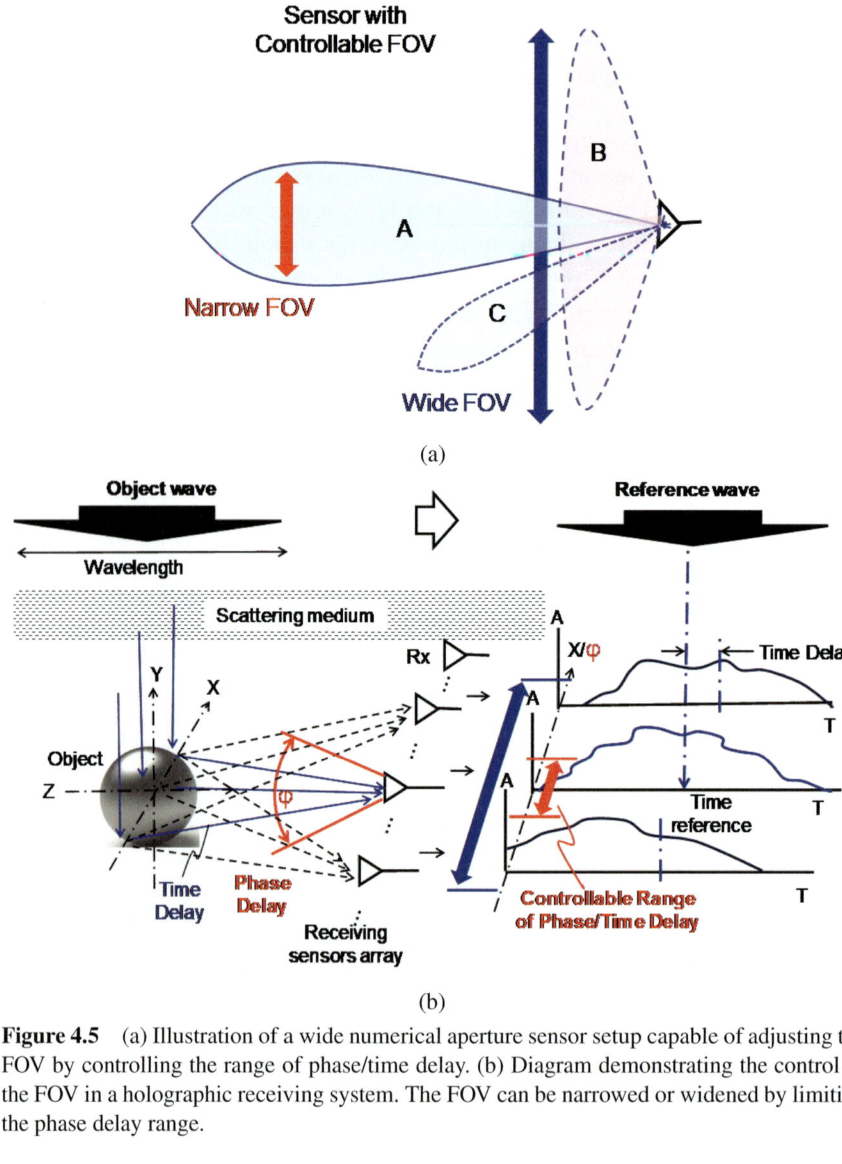

Figure 4.5 (a) Illustration of a wide numerical aperture sensor setup capable of adjusting the FOV by controlling the range of phase/time delay. (b) Diagram demonstrating the control of the FOV in a holographic receiving system. The FOV can be narrowed or widened by limiting the phase delay range.

can optimize the processing of visual information, reducing unnecessary data capture and focusing resources on areas of interest. Dynamic FOV control facilitates efficient data handling, particularly in environments where data transfer speeds are limited. This capability ensures that critical visual information is captured and processed without overwhelming the system.

Emulating the human eye's ability to adjust FOV, the system provides a more intuitive and effective imaging experience, enhancing its usability in various applications.

Controllable FOV in remote detection and imaging systems offers a significant advancement in imaging technology. By utilizing wide numerical aperture sensors and managing phase/time delays, the system can dynamically adjust its FOV, providing both broad coverage and focused detail as needed. This capability, implemented through digital FOV coding programs, ensures efficient data processing and improved imaging resolution, making the system versatile and adaptable to diverse operational requirements.

4.2.3 Controllable depth of field

For optical systems, the depth of field (DOF) of a lens refers to its ability to maintain a desired level of image quality (spatial frequency at a specified contrast) without the need for refocusing when the object moves closer to or farther from the plane of best focus. This concept is applicable not only to objects with simple geometries but also to those with complex features or varying heights [Edmund Optics].

In systems using electromagnetic waves, such as radio and microwave frequencies, the DOF is inversely proportional to the aperture size of the sensor array. A larger aperture size results in a smaller DOF, meaning that the system can maintain a high level of image quality over a smaller range of distances from the sensor array to the object [2].

The wavelength of the electromagnetic waves used also affects the DOF. Longer wavelengths typically result in a greater DOF, allowing for a wider range of object distances to be in focus. Advanced RF imaging systems can employ adaptive focusing techniques, dynamically adjusting the effective aperture size or the focal plane to optimize the DOF based on the specific requirements of the imaging task.

Implementing a variable aperture design allows the system to adjust the aperture size dynamically, optimizing the DOF based on the object's distance and the desired image resolution. Using real-time data from the sensor array, the system can adjust the focal plane to maintain focus on objects at varying distances. This can be achieved through electronic focusing mechanisms that modify the phase and time delay of the received signals.

Deploying multiple sensor arrays with different fixed aperture sizes can provide a composite image with varying DOFs. This approach allows the system to capture high-resolution images of objects at different depths simultaneously. The ability to control the DOF dynamically provides greater flexibility in imaging diverse objects with varying distances and geometries. By optimizing the DOF for specific imaging tasks, the system can maintain high image quality across a range of object distances, enhancing the overall effectiveness of the imaging process.

The capability to adjust the DOF makes the system suitable for a wide range of applications, from biomedical imaging to remote sensing and underground object detection.

4.2.4 Control of vision direction

The direction of vision in the holographic remote detection system can be controlled by adjusting the reference time across all sensors simultaneously. This method allows for precise control over the vision direction without the need for mechanical movement or adjustments. The principle is based on the superposition of scattered and diffracted frequency components reflected from the object, which are received by wide numerical aperture sensors [3–8].

Controlling vision direction with reference time presented in Figure 4.6. Each sensor in the array receives scattered and diffracted components from the object. By adjusting the reference time for each sensor, the system can control the phase and time alignment of the received signals. This adjustment shifts the focus direction of the system, allowing it to "look" in different directions without physically moving the sensors.

The scattered and diffracted frequency components are superimposed relative to the adjusted reference times for each sensor. This superposition process effectively changes the direction of the combined wavefronts, thereby controlling the vision direction. The use of wide numerical aperture sensors ensures that a broad range of angles and frequencies are captured. This capability enhances the system's ability to control the vision direction accurately.

Simultaneous reference time control is provided by synchronizing the reference time adjustments across all sensors, the system can maintain coherence and alignment in the received signals. This synchronization is crucial for accurate direction control. Advanced algorithms are used to calculate the necessary reference time adjustments for each sensor based on the desired vision direction. These calculations take into account the relative positions of the sensors and the characteristics of the received signals.

Real-time processing capabilities are essential to dynamically adjust the reference times and control the vision direction. This requires high-speed

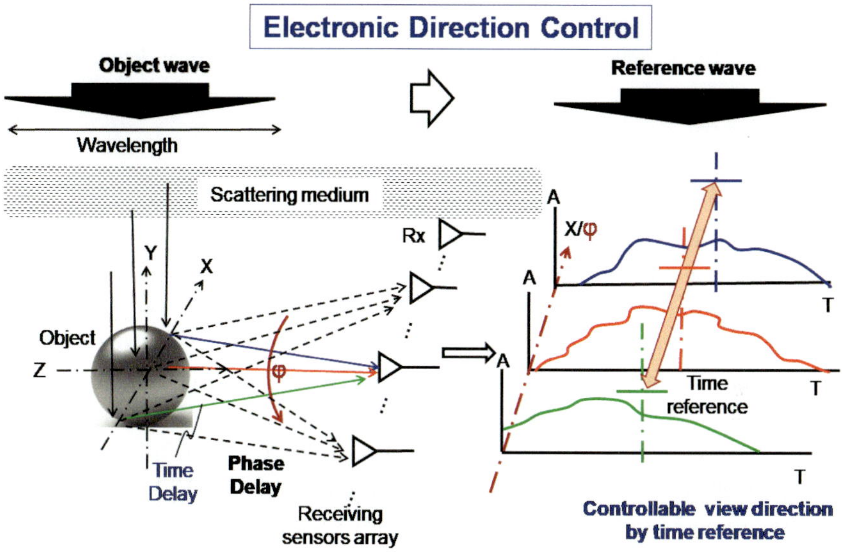

Figure 4.6 Control of time reference simultaneous in all sensors is providing control of vision direction. The phase delay of all scattered and diffracted frequency components and their superposition them relative to different reference times provide different vision directions of the system.

processors and efficient data handling to manage the adjustments without delay.

The ability to control vision direction electronically eliminates the need for mechanical movement, reducing wear and tear and increasing system reliability. Electronic control of vision direction allows for rapid adjustments, enabling the system to quickly adapt to changing scenarios and targets.

The system can seamlessly switch between different vision directions, providing comprehensive coverage and improved situational awareness. Without the need for mechanical components to control direction, the system can be more compact and lightweight, making it suitable for various applications, including portable and mobile systems.

Controlling the vision direction in a holographic remote detection system through reference time adjustments provides a powerful and flexible method for enhancing imaging capabilities. By synchronizing these adjustments across wide numerical aperture sensors, the system achieves precise direction control without mechanical movement. This approach offers significant advantages in terms of speed, accuracy, and reliability, making it an effective solution for a wide range of imaging applications. The implementation of this technology can lead to advancements in fields such as surveillance, medical imaging, and remote sensing, where dynamic and accurate vision direction is crucial.

4.2.5 Electronic focus control

Electronic focus control in a remote detection holographic system can be achieved by simultaneously adjusting the reference time across all sensors. This method allows precise control over the focal plane without the need for mechanical adjustments or moving parts. The principle involves manipulating the phase and time alignment of the received signals, which changes the focus of the system. The diagram for focus control is presented in Figure 4.7.

By controlling the reference time for all sensors in the array simultaneously, the system can adjust the focus to different depths or planes. This adjustment aligns the phases of the received signals to focus on specific areas of interest. The use of sensors with wide numerical apertures ensures that a

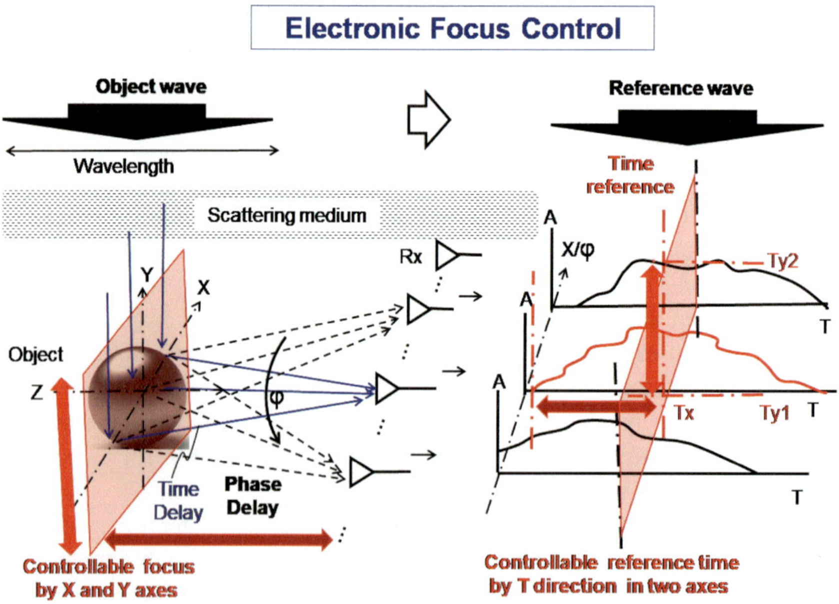

Figure 4.7 Electronic focus control in holographic remote detection system. To control focus on a flat surface slicing object by *X* and *Y* axes at some distance from the antenna array by axis *Z*, we need to adjust the reference time in all sensors simultaneously by axes *X* and *Y*. Reference time by axis *X* shown on the diagram as *Tx*. Reference times by axis *Y* is shown on the diagram as a flat surface between *Ty*1 and *Ty*2.

broad range of angles and frequencies are captured. This capability enhances the system's ability to adjust focus accurately. The scattered and diffracted frequency components are superimposed relative to the adjusted reference times for each sensor. This superposition process changes the focal plane of the combined wavefronts, thereby controlling the focus of the system. The system needs to be calibrated to establish a baseline reference time for all sensors, ensuring that the initial focus is correctly set. Reference time adjustment is provided simultaneously across all sensors to change the focus. This adjustment brings the phases of the received signals into alignment for the desired focal plane. Algorithms can be used to calculate the necessary reference time adjustments based on the desired focus depth or plane. These calculations consider the relative positions of the sensors and the characteristics of the received signals. Implementing real-time processing allows dynamically adjusting the reference times and control of the focus. High-speed processors and efficient data handling are essential to manage these adjustments without delay.

Providing electronic control of focus eliminates the need for mechanical adjustments, reducing wear and tear and increasing system reliability. Electronic focus control allows for rapid adjustments, enabling the system to quickly refocus on different areas of interest. The system can seamlessly switch focus between different planes, providing comprehensive coverage and improved situational awareness. Without the need for mechanical components to control focus, the system can be more compact and lightweight, making it suitable for various applications, including portable and mobile systems.

Electronic focus control in a remote detection holographic system through reference time adjustments provides a powerful and flexible method for enhancing imaging capabilities. By synchronizing these adjustments across wide numerical aperture sensors, the system achieves precise focus control without mechanical movement. This approach offers significant advantages in terms of speed, accuracy, and reliability, making it an effective solution for a wide range of imaging applications. The implementation of this technology can lead to advancements in fields such as surveillance, medical imaging, and remote sensing, where dynamic and accurate focus control is crucial.

4.2.6 Forming of object spectrum signature in high-scattering medium

In a high-scattering medium, signals scattered and diffracted by objects are captured by a holographic array of sensors with a wide numerical aperture.

This setup ensures coverage of entire objects or multiple objects, facilitating the reception of scattered and diffracted frequency components that describe the diffraction pattern and its spatial/angular distribution. The process involves several critical steps, from signal reception to the formation of object spectrum signatures, enabling precise control and filtering for various functions (Figure 4.8) [3, 4].

The holographic array of sensors with wide numerical aperture need to be applied to capture scattered and diffracted signals to form objects and medium spectrum signatures. Direct digitization is applied to convert the received signals into real-time digital holograms in the time domain. Fourier transform is applied to convert digitally recorded diffraction patterns from the time domain to the frequency domain, enabling detailed analysis and manipulation of frequency components. Field of view, direction, and focus control are adjusting the system's vision parameters by manipulating specific groups of frequency components. Filters can help to separates spectrum signatures of objects from those of the scattering medium and isolates frequency components corresponding to the object's shape, size, and dielectric properties. Filters also can help to identify and suppresses unwanted signals, enhancing the clarity of the object's spectral signature.

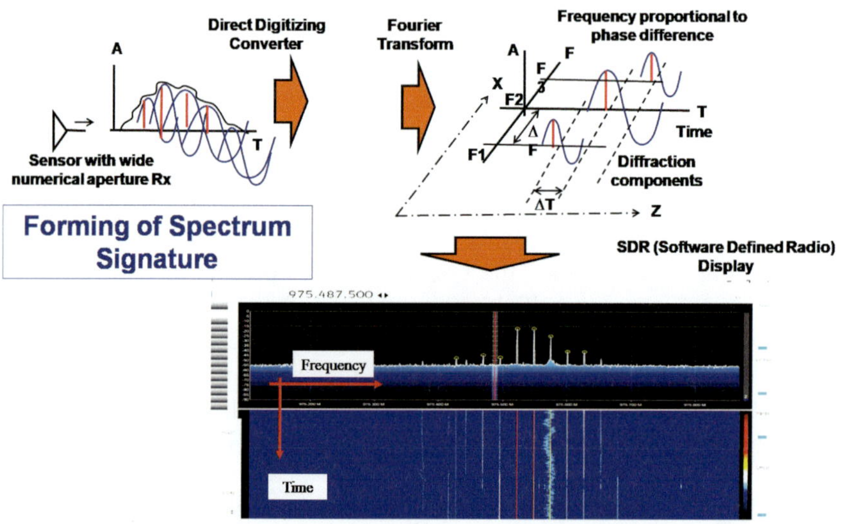

Figure 4.8 Recording of spectrum signatures of object in one sensor channel. Waterfall presents real-time changes in frequency components, which can represent the shape, size, and dielectric properties of the object or scattering medium.

By controlling and filtering frequency components, the system can dynamically adjust the field of view, direction, and focus, allowing for more flexible and precise imaging. The separation of spectrum signatures and identification of object-specific frequency components improve the accuracy of object recognition, even in high-scattering environments. Effective suppression of interference, rereflections, and noise signals ensures that the resulting spectrum signatures are clear and reliable. The ability to isolate and analyze frequency components related to an object's physical properties (shape, size, dielectric properties) allows for detailed and comprehensive object analysis.

The formation of object spectrum signatures in a high-scattering medium through advanced RF imaging techniques provides significant advantages in object recognition and imaging resolution. By leveraging the capabilities of wide numerical aperture sensors and real-time digital holography, coupled with Fourier transform and precise control of frequency components, this method offers robust solutions for overcoming challenges posed by high-scattering environments. The outlined process enhances the ability to detect, recognize, and analyze objects with high accuracy, making it a powerful tool in various applications, from medical imaging to remote sensing and beyond.

4.2.7 Real-time visualization and digital recording of spectrum signatures

The proposed technique for real-time visualization and digital recording of spectrum signatures significantly enhances the analysis of objects and scattering mediums. This advanced method provides powerful analytic tools that facilitate detailed examinations of various properties, allowing for precise control and filtration of frequency components. These capabilities are essential for applications requiring high-resolution imaging and accurate object recognition in complex environments.

Real-time visualization and immediate analysis enables the real-time examination of spectrum signatures, providing instant feedback on object and medium properties. It allows for on-the-fly modifications to the imaging process, ensuring optimal data collection. Digital recording and comprehensive data storage facilitate the storage of vast amounts of data, preserving detailed records of frequency components for future analysis and enabling the replay and review of recorded data, supporting thorough post-processing analysis.

Analytic tools can be applied for object and medium analysis. Different groups of frequency components represent various properties such as size, shape, and dielectric properties of the object. These can be pre-tested and filtered for automatic applications. Similarly, the scattering medium properties can be analyzed and filtered to enhance imaging accuracy. Figure 4.9 presents a diagram of real-time visualization and digital recording in the system.

The system can identify and suppress interference, re-reflected signals, and signals received from incorrect directions or with incorrect parameters and enhance signal clarity by filtering out noise and unwanted signals, the clarity and reliability of the spectrum signatures are significantly improved.

High-resolution visualization technique can be applied for medical imaging, which enables detailed imaging of biological tissues and improves diagnostic capabilities. It reduces interference from surrounding tissues and other signals, enhancing image quality. It facilitates precise mapping of terrains by analyzing the frequency components of reflected signals. It provides interference management, suppressing unwanted signals from environmental factors, ensuring clearer data collection.

Material property analysis allows for the detailed examination of material properties, identifying defects or irregularities. Real-time monitoring can

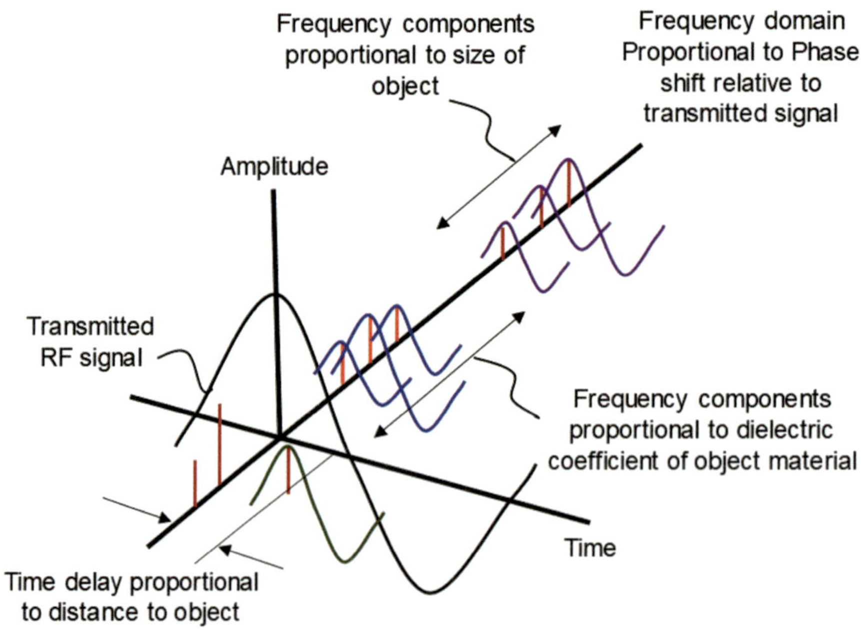

Figure 4.9 Groups of frequency components after transferring to frequency domain representing size and dielectric properties of object and distance to object.

support continuous monitoring of industrial processes, providing immediate feedback on material conditions.

Enhanced object recognition improves the detection and identification of objects in security applications, even in cluttered environments. It adapts to changing conditions in real-time, maintaining optimal surveillance performance.

The ability to dynamically adjust and filter frequency components ensures that the system can adapt to various applications, from medical imaging to industrial testing and security surveillance. This approach represents a significant advancement in the field of RF imaging, offering robust solutions for challenging high-scattering environments.

The integration of real-time visualization and digital recording of spectrum signatures offers a comprehensive solution for analyzing objects and scattering mediums. By providing advanced analytic tools and capabilities for interference management, this technique significantly enhances the accuracy and resolution of imaging systems. The ability to dynamically adjust and filter frequency components ensures that the system can adapt to various applications, from medical imaging to industrial testing and security surveillance. This approach represents a significant advancement in the field of RF imaging, offering robust solutions for challenging high-scattering environments.

4.3 Testing of Some Human-like Vision System Applications

4.3.1 Vision human health and biomedical application

The proposed technology providing human-like vision allows achieving precise positioning, shape determination, and object recognition within high-scattering mediums. Utilizing an array of staring electromagnetic sensors characterized by a wide numerical aperture, the technology provides simultaneous and high-accuracy information about entire objects. Low-power radiofrequency electromagnetic signals, known for their outstanding penetration capabilities through high-scattering mediums such as the human body or biomedical liquids, can be employed in wearable devices, offering clear contrast for various tissues, bones, and anomalies (Figure 4.10).

The integrated wide numerical aperture sensors, in conjunction with multi-channel direct processing and digitizing receivers, enable the detection of diffraction patterns with angular distribution in the near-field zone.

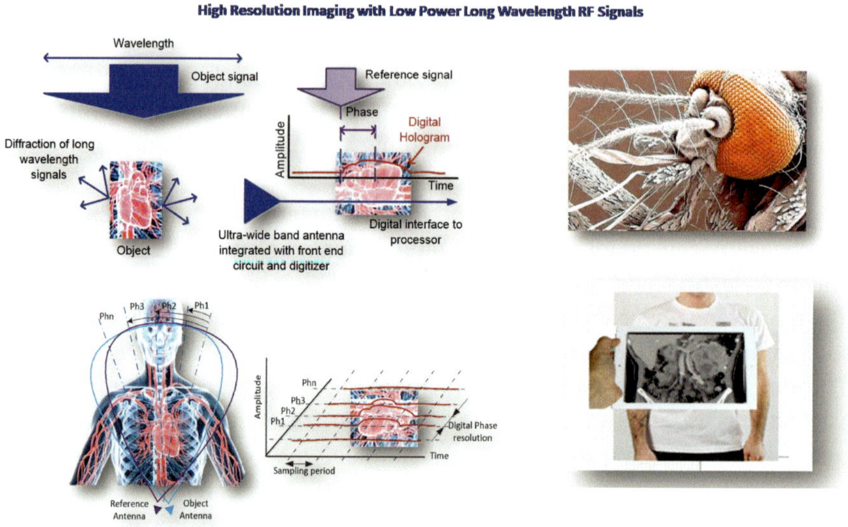

Figure 4.10 Nature-inspired high-resolution imaging system can be applied for preliminary estimation of patient state. Systems do not require high-accuracy expensive optics, reliable for application in harsh conditions, and can be used in different areas, including rescue or military operations.

Overlapping sensor patterns facilitate the implementation of simple and fast monopulse one-step algorithms, ensuring high-accuracy amplitude and phase processing. These patterns also contribute to suppressing interference and background signals, which enhances reliable object recognition based on spectrum signatures. This innovation enables the detection of objects irrespective of their spatial orientation, particularly for objects smaller than the irradiating wavelength. The proposed remote digital holographic system has been successfully applied for the measurement of micro-Doppler signals corresponding to human breathing and heartbeats. The system demonstrated its capability by detecting human breathing and heartbeats through a 30-inch concrete wall, as presented in Figure 4.11.

The testing setup for remote object recognition through 30 inches of concrete wall relies on analyzing spectrum signatures. The spectrum signature comprises a group of informative diffraction components that contain information about identified objects, as well as a group of non-informative diffraction components, as shown in Figure 4.12.

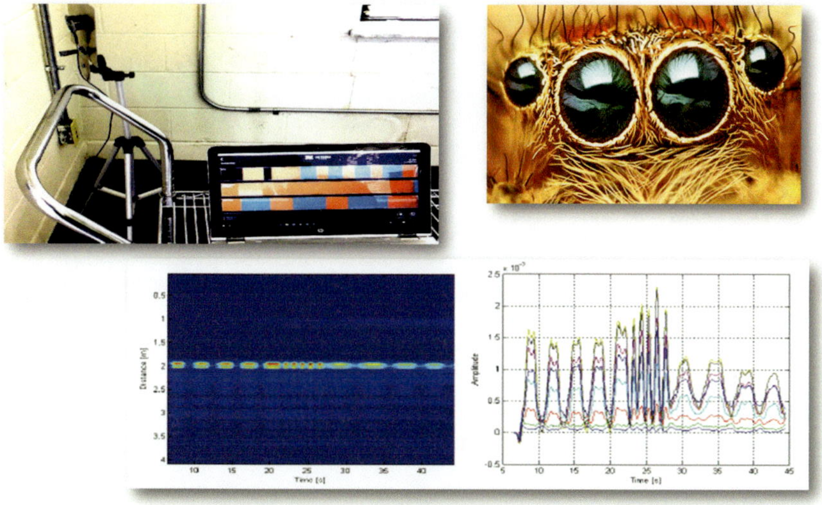

Figure 4.11 The digital holographic system testing for remote through the 30-inch concrete wall, measurement of micro-Doppler signals corresponding to human breathing and heart beating.

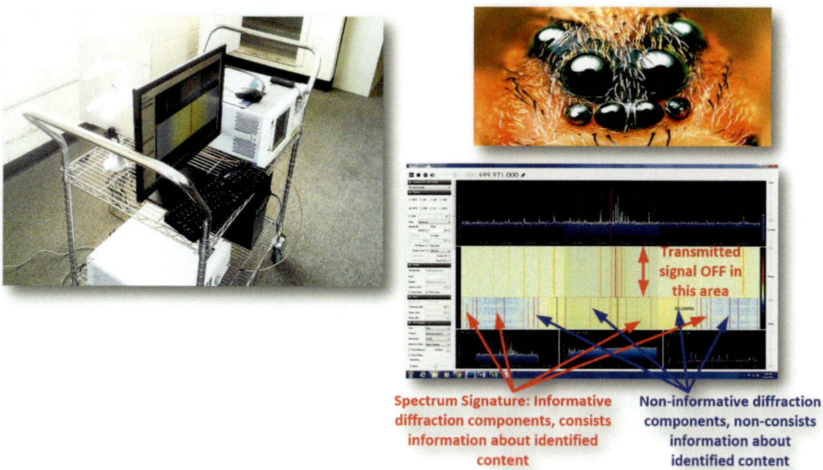

Figure 4.12 The digital holographic system testing for remote through the 30-inch concrete wall, measurement of spectrum signature of the object consists of identified content. On display presented spectrum components representing information related to object and components representing background wall and sources of outside signals.

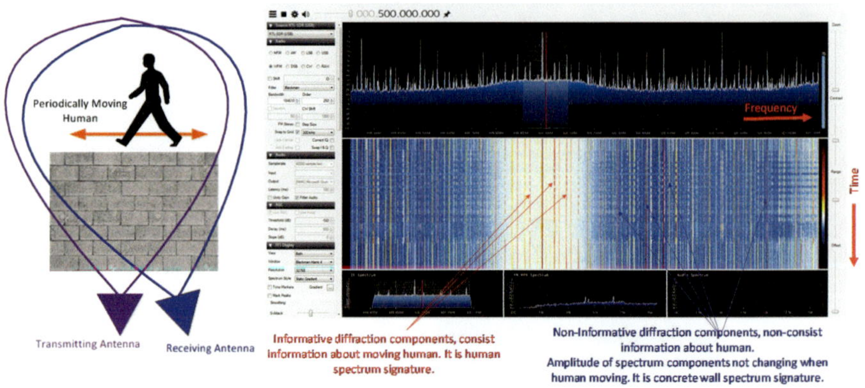

Figure 4.13 The digital holographic system testing for remote through the 30-inch concrete wall, measurement of moving human by spectrum signature consisting of micro-Doppler time modulation.

This spectrum signature also includes signals from outside sources, such as broadcast stations and Wi-Fi systems, as well as diffraction components corresponding to background noise, including the concrete wall. The movement of a human was detected through a 30-inch concrete wall at a distance of up to 20 meters, using this spectrum signature. The human spectrum signature features time modulation corresponding to the movement of human body parts, such as hands and legs (Figure 4.13).

This innovative setup demonstrates the capability of the system to identify and track moving objects in high-scattering mediums by analyzing their unique spectrum signatures, even in challenging environments like behind thick concrete walls.

4.3.2 Small sense and avoid system application

Small sense and avoid (SAA) systems for micro and small unmanned aerial systems (UAS) are essential to prevent collisions with obstacles and other aircraft. These systems enable drones to "see" their surroundings and maneuver through tight spaces with agility. Unlike optical or infrared (IR) systems, Doppler radar can function effectively in harsh conditions, such as at dusk, in rain, and in snow. Additionally, compared to ultrasound-based systems, Doppler radar can better detect small-sized obstacles like wires and offers a sensing range from a few inches to several miles.

The proposed SAA system consists of Doppler radar modules and an array of directional antennas distributed around the drone's perimeter, ensuring comprehensive coverage of the entire sky. The SAA system is capable of operating in low visibility conditions such as rain, snow, and fog. It provides detection in wide sensing range from a few inches to several miles, accommodating various obstacle sizes.

The SAA is superior at identifying small obstacles, such as wires, foliage, organic liquids, and different dielectric materials that may not be detected by other sensor types. Some samples of materials that can be detected and recognized are presented above in Chapter 3.

Directional antennas distributed around the drone perimeter ensure 360-degree coverage, minimizing blind spots. Measures relative velocity between the drone and objects, enhancing obstacle avoidance capabilities.

The SAA normally comprises multiple distributed transceiver antenna modules (TAM), which also detect Doppler micro-motions. These modules emit radio waves and analyze the reflected signals to determine the presence and speed of objects. Directional antennas with overlap antenna patterns are strategically positioned around the drone to provide all-around coverage, ensuring no blind spots. The signal processing unit processes the radar data to identify obstacles and calculate their relative speed and distance. Control system integrated with transceiver module by digital interface. The processed data is fed into the drone's control system, enabling real-time maneuvering decisions to avoid collisions.

TAMs are placed to maximize coverage, ensuring detection from all directions. High-speed processors analyze radar data in real time, facilitating immediate obstacle detection and avoidance maneuvers. AI-based algorithms adapt to changing environments and obstacles, optimizing avoidance strategies.

SAA can be applied for:

- Urban navigation – maneuvering through buildings, power lines, and other structures.
- Search and rescue – operating in diverse environments, including dense forests and mountainous terrains.
- Delivery drones – ensuring safe navigation in populated areas.
- Military operations – enhancing situational awareness and avoiding obstacles in complex environments (Figure 4.14).

By integrating Doppler radar modules with directional antennas, small and micro UAS can achieve reliable and effective sense and avoid capabilities, significantly enhancing their operational safety and versatility in various challenging conditions [9–22].

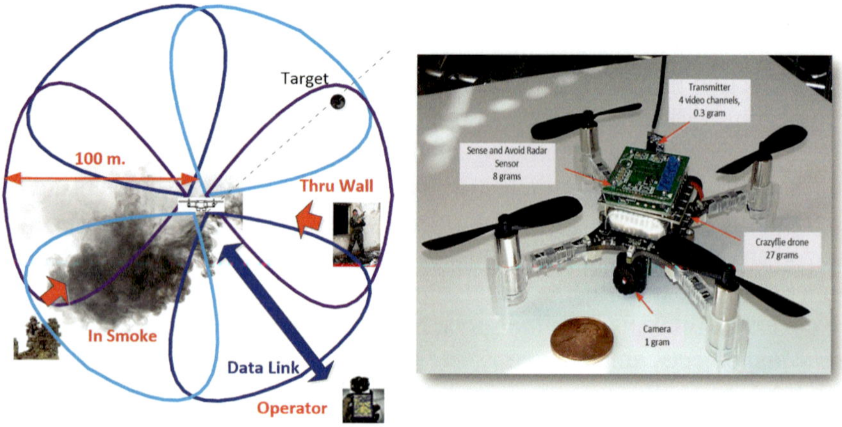

Figure 4.14 The nano-drone with RF remote detection and recognition through smoke and through wall radar.

4.3.3 Multi-function radar-mode sense and avoid system design

The multi-function radar-mode SAA system for small drones can combine several features to ensure robust obstacle detection and avoidance and can include automatic dependent surveillance-broadcast (ADS-B). ADS-B is an aviation surveillance technology and a form of electronic conspicuity in which an aircraft (or other airborne vehicles such as drones approved to fit "ADS-B Out") determines its position via satellite navigation or other sensors and periodically broadcasts its position and other related data, enabling it to be tracked [Wikipedia]. Such a combination allows sensing and avoiding both cooperative and non-cooperative aircrafts (Figure 4.15).

This system uses an array of directional antennas coupled to radar sensors, distributed around the UAS to provide comprehensive coverage. The system operates by transmitting CW microwave signals, detecting Doppler shifts in reflected signals, and processing this data to generate avoidance commands for the drone's autopilot. At the same time transceiver can be applied for transmitting/receiving ADS-B messages. Implementing Doppler radar for SAA in small drones significantly enhances their operational capabilities by providing reliable, real-time obstacle detection and avoidance. This technology allows drones to navigate safely and autonomously in complex environments, expanding their potential applications and operational areas.

SAA radar modules are engineered to detect obstacles and provide directional data while simultaneously generating an alarm signal if an obstacle

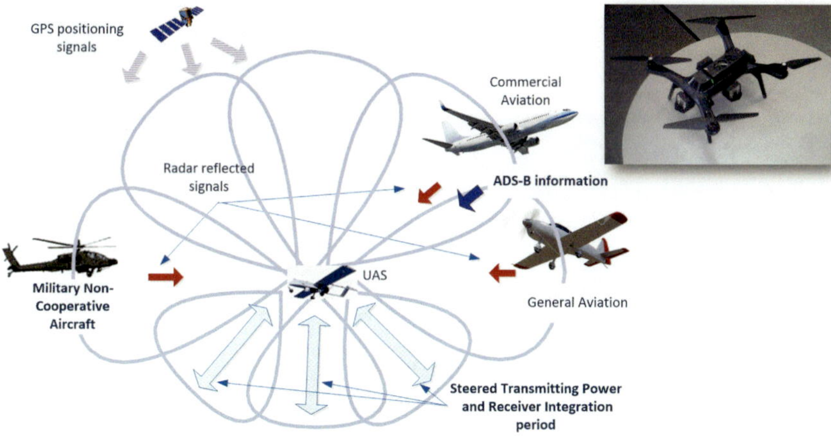

Figure 4.15 The multi-function sense and avoid system for navigation, sense, and avoidance cooperative and non-cooperative aircraft, ground communications.

enters the SAA system's adjustable "Protection Border." This alarm signal prompts the drone's autopilot to execute an avoidance maneuver automatically. A series of SAA radar modules has been developed, each tailored for drones of varying sizes and applications. These modules differ in their range, angle of view, and transmitting power to cater to specific needs. Key features of the proposed Doppler radar micro SAA system include:

- Direction and distance measurement. The modules provide precise direction to the obstacle, aiding in accurate and timely avoidance actions.
- Adjustable protection border. The system's protection border can be adjusted to define the critical range within which the drone must react to avoid collisions.
- Alarm signal generation. Upon detecting an obstacle within the protection border, the modules generate an alarm signal that triggers the drone's autopilot to initiate avoidance maneuvers.

The micro SAA system's versatility allows it to be used across various drone types and sizes. Its ability to function in diverse environmental conditions, including low visibility and adverse weather, makes it a valuable addition to any drone navigation system. Whether for hobbyist drones, commercial delivery drones, or specialized applications like search and rescue operations, this system enhances safety and operational efficiency.

Figure 4.16 Testing of sense and avoid radar system distributed around small drone perimeter presented in videos [22] and demonstrated at airshows in Paris, France, and Farnborough, UK.

By integrating these SAA radar modules into small unmanned aircraft, drones gain enhanced situational awareness and obstacle avoidance capabilities. The lightweight, low-power, and cost-effective design ensures that the system can be widely adopted, significantly improving the safety and functionality of drones in various applications. Some SAA test pictures and videos are presented in Figure 4.16 [9–22].

Conclusion

The proposed novel technology for image recognition with human-like, electronically scalable accuracy leverages contemporary digital holographic methods and monopulse multi-channel processing signals from nature-inspired directional sensor arrays. This technology involves an AI fabric that retrains imaging models for electronic control of range, direction, area of observation, and imaging recognition accuracy.

By applying digital holographic processing to signals from wide numerical aperture sensor arrays, this technology addresses the imaging resolution challenge by shifting the diffraction limit from spatial pixel size to the time domain. The resolution is determined by the minimal digital sampling and phase measurement steps, offering an advantage with relatively long radio and microwave wavelengths.

Key aspects of the technology include overcoming pixel size limitations. Traditional techniques are often limited by diffraction limit, determined by the minimum pixel size. Digital holography, however, allows for imaging resolution determined by minimum phase measurements and signal sampling steps, enabling the capture of finer details and making vision resolution electronically controllable and scalable.

Utilization of long-wavelength radio frequency signals, known for their excellent penetration capabilities, enables high-resolution imaging and recognition, especially in high-scattering conditions. Information remains invariant to the object's spatial position when radio and microwave wavelengths are long relative to the object's size, ensuring robustness in recognizing objects regardless of their location.

The monopulse multi-channel signal processing method significantly reduces computational complexity. Simple one-step algorithms for object recognition and decision-making enhance the system's efficiency.

Versatility across electromagnetic spectra is not limited to optical wavelengths and can be applied across various electromagnetic spectra, making it suitable for applications ranging from interferometric microscopy to health monitoring and astronomical telescopes.

The innovative aspects and potential applications of this technology promise significant advancements in object recognition in high-scattering mediums using radio and microwave frequencies. The integration of the angular spectrum of diffracted and scattered components into Fresnel coherent diffraction imaging enables real-time digital recording of distribution patterns, offering a robust and versatile solution for high-resolution imaging and object recognition.

References

[1] D. Georgiev, " What is the maximum human field of vision?" Quora, 2024. [Online] Available https://www.quora.com/what-is-the-maximum-human-field-of-vision [Accessed January 12, 2023].

[2] G. Hollows, N. James, "Depth of Field and Depth of Focus," Edmund Optics, Imaging resource guide, 2024. [Online] Available https://edmundoptics.com/knowledge-center [Accessed January 12, 2024].

[3] P. Molchanov, *"Seeing Invisible: Advanced Antenna Arrays,"* River Publishers, ISBN: 9781003476559, February 2024. [Online] Available www.riverpublishers.com ,[Accassed April 12, 2024].

[4] P. Molchanov, "Multi-Antenna Array for All Space Communications," 2024 IEEE *Radio Wireless Week (RWW),* San Antonio, TX, USA, January 21, 2024.

[5] S. Harman "A comparison of staring radars with scanning radars for UAV detection: introduction of the Alarm TM staring radar," 2015, *European Radar Conference (EURAD), EUMA*, Sep. 2015, 185-188.

[6] S. A. Harman, (Aveillant Ltd., Cambridge, U.K.)," *Holographic Radar Development,*" 2021-02-07, [Online] Available www.microwavejournal .com [Accessed April 12, 2023].

[7] J. Goodman, W. Joseph, R. Lawrence, "*Digital image formation from electronically detected holograms," Applied Physics Letters*. 11 (3): 1967, 77–79.

[8] U. Schnars, W. Jüptner, "*Digital Holography,*" Springer. ISBN 9783642060182. 2005.

[9] P. Molchanov, "All Digital Radar Architecture," Paper 9248-11, SPIE Security+Defense Conference, Amsterdam, September 25, 2014.

[10] P. Molchanov, O. Asmolova, "Sense and Avoid Radar for Micro-/Nano Robots," (Invited Paper), SPIE Security+Defense Conference, Amsterdam, September 24, 2014.

[11] P. Molchanov, O. Asmolova, "Fly Eye Radar or Micro-Radar Sensor Technology," SPIE Security+Defense, Session C31, Sensors, Control, Communications, Technologies for Homeland Security and Homeland Defense XIII, Proc. Of SPIE Vol.9074 907405, May 6, 2014.

[12] P. Molchanov, "New Protected GPS Antenna Technology," Joint Navigation Conference 2014, Orlando, FL, Session C2 Antenna Technologies and Interference Mitigation. June 17, 2014.

[13] P. Molchanov, V. Contarino, "Directional antenna array for communications, control and data link protection," SPIE 2013 Defense + Security. Session 9, Communication, Control, and Enabling Technologies, Paper 8711-31, April 30, 2013.

[14] P. Molchanov, V. Contarino, "New Distributed Radar Technology based on UAV or UGV Application," SPIE 2013 Defense + Security. Session 6, MIMO Radar, Paper 8714-27, April 30, 2013.

[15] P. Molchanov, V. Contarino, O. Asmolova, "Protected GPS Directional Antenna Array," Colorado Springs, JSDE/ION Joint Navigation Conference 2012, Session C7: Navigation Warfare: GPS in Military Applications II, June, 2012.

[16] V. Contarino, S. Young, P. Molchanov, "Collision Avoidance Demonstration for UAS,", Canada, Ottawa, Nov. 6-12, 2012.

[17] R. Healing, V. Contarino, P. Molchanov, "Mini Sense and Avoid Radar," Small UAS Symposium, Johns Hopkins University APL, June, 2011.
[18] P. Molchanov, R. Healing, O. Asmolova,"Radar-mode sense and avoid system." Conf. Unmanned Systems, Canada. Nova Scotia, Canada, K1P1B1, Nov. 7-10, 2011.
[19] P. Molchanov,V. Contarino, O. Asmolova, "Array of Directional Antennas for GPS Anti-jam, Anti-spoof Protection," San Diego, ION International Technical Meeting, Session B1 Receiver and antenna Technologies, January 28-30, 2013.
[20] V. Contarino, P. Molchanov, R. Healing, O. Asmolova, "UAV radar system of low observable targets," Conf. Unmanned Systems, Canada. Nova Scotia, Canada, K1P1B1, Nov. 7-10, 2011.
[21] P. Molchanov, V Contarino, "Multi-beam Antenna Array for Protecting GPS Receivers from Jamming and Spoofing Signals," U.S. Patent and Trademark Office (USPTO) application, (reference USPTO EFS-Web Receipt 13562313 dated 31 July 20, 2012.
[22] Video, [Online] Available https://youtu.be/2BvJWGd4raU [Accessed April 2024].

5

Artificial Eye

Introduction

It is obvious that a nature-inspired vision system, which provides new advanced possibilities of limitless controllable resolution, human-like scalable range, focus, direction, and field of view control, can be applied not only for technical systems but also for human artificial vision, particularly for artificial eye design. The new artificial eye can be applied as a human vision system which will avoid any human body or brain surgery or chip implementation. Also, it will provide a few advances compared to regular human vision, like an extension of visible EM waves frequency range, extension range and field of view, and vision of concealed objects. The application of simple metal RF antenna arrays instead of expensive precision semiconductor light sensors will increase sensor reliability in any environmental conditions and make the system more simple and inexpensive.

5.1 Artificial Vision, Prior Art

Artificial vision can be divided depending on its relation to humans into two parts: *Human artificial vision* and *technical artificial vision* including *computer vision*. Human artificial vision is related to vision provided directly or through some sensors interface to the human brain. Computer vision focuses on analyzing and understanding digital images, which means extracting the maximum possible imaging information. In contrast, human artificial vision usually does not need to analyze all the details of the image, but only those that consist of information about objects and trigger a particular action. Automated Imaging Association (AIA) proposes to divide artificial vision into industrial and non-industrial applications where a combination

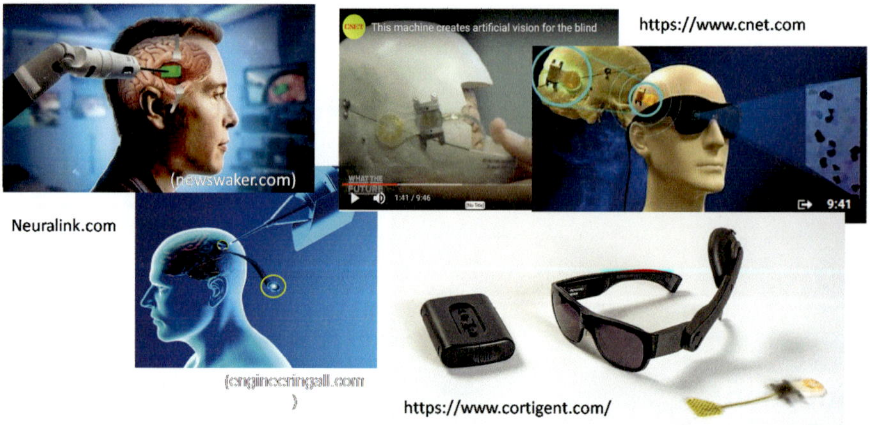

Figure 5.1 Most of artificial human vision systems developed by different companies are requiring risky brain surgery to implant a chip directly into the brain.

of hardware and software provides operational guidance to devices in the execution of their functions based on image capture and processing [1].

The most known human artificial vision systems were developed by Neurolink Inc. [2], Cortigent Inc. [3], and UT Southwestern Medical Center [4] are presented in Figure 5.1. Light hits the eye and passes through the cornea, the lens, and the outer and middle layers of the eye. When light reaches the back layer of the eye, the retina cells called photoreceptors, where light is converted into electrical signals. These discrete discrete electrical signals travel through the optic nerve to the brain, which interprets those signals as images. The eyes can't communicate with the brain Bottom of Form without an intact retina or optic nerve. The artificial eye can be used by many people with total or partial blindness. These types of devices allow bypassing the eye and optic nerve completely, sending information straight to the brain. Because of this, they have the potential to address any cause of blindness, whether due to eye disease or trauma.

The artificial visual system developed by Bionic Eye System [5] also consists of a wearable device and visual implant chip. It operates by translating images from a camera mounted on an eyeglass frame into electrical signals stimulating the nerves via electrodes placed behind the retina to deliver visual information to the brain. The camera captures images in real time and sends image information to the processing unit. Then encoded signals transfer to

Figure 5.2 Cameras or visual sensors in artificial vision systems can be designed as eye imitations or built into glasses. Resolution provided by sensor systems is usually limited by a number of sensors and limited by technology possibilities.

the implant via a wireless interface located under the scalp. Camera can be installed on the eyeglass frames (Figure 5.2).

These devices could provide blind people with a crude sense of sight but still require brain surgery and an implanted microchip directly in the brain. Humans require risky brain surgery to get a visual prosthesis for the brain implant for vision.

The goal of the Stanford Artificial Retina Project [6] is to develop an advanced artificial retina: an electronic implant that will restore vision to people blinded by incurable retinal disease. The project focuses on an innovative combination of basic and applied research to create a unique device capable of closely mimicking normal retinal function. In contrast to the other approaches, the aim of this project is to reproduce the precise retinal code at a cellular resolution with cell-type specificity, resulting in high-fidelity artificial vision (Figure 5.3). The other artificial retina project is the Second Sight Argus II [7]. With it, people with certain types of blindness can detect large objects, the presence of people or cars, and sometimes oversized numbers or letters. Several other groups and companies are pursuing investigational efforts to develop retinal prosthetics, including Pixium Vision (France) [8], Bionic Eye Technologies (US) [5], and Nanoretina (Israel) [9].

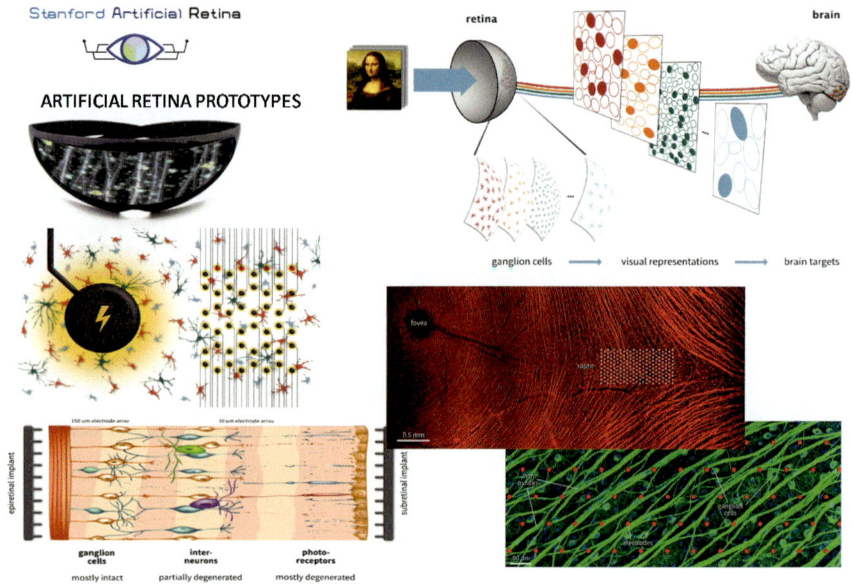

Figure 5.3 Stanford artificial retina project and other development retina projects including artificial implants.

5.2 Artificial Eye: Nature-inspired Concept

The target of the proposed artificial eye development is to avoid human brain surgery, retina implants, or other surgeries and create a system that can be used as regular glasses for blind humans or humans with partial losses or limited vision. Proposed below is an artificial eye RF system based on a nature-inspired fly eye concept. It consists of multiple directional wide numerical aperture antennas with overlap antenna patterns (Figure 5.4). Also, the proposed artificial eyes can be used for imitation of human eyes. From that side, artificial eyes can be applied for enhancing human vision, like extension of range, field of view, and vision of concealed objects.

Proposed fly eye RF radar based on the processing of reflected from object wavefront signals recorded as a digital hologram with non-scanning, non-switching wide area covering antenna array with reference to processor time. Overlapping of antenna patterns can prove high-resolution imaging by application of the monopulse method of processing [10–16]. Multi-axis distribution of overlap antennas and application of reference antennas provides maximum information about object shape for better imaging (Figure 5.5).

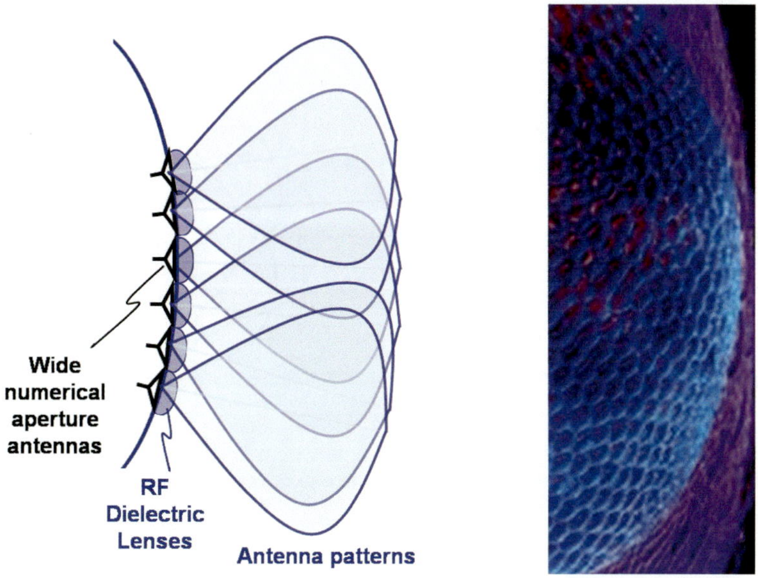

Figure 5.4 Nature-inspired fly eye RF radar concept with multiple directional wide numerical aperture antennas applied for creating an artificial eye surface. Micro-lenses are applied for extending antenna apertures.

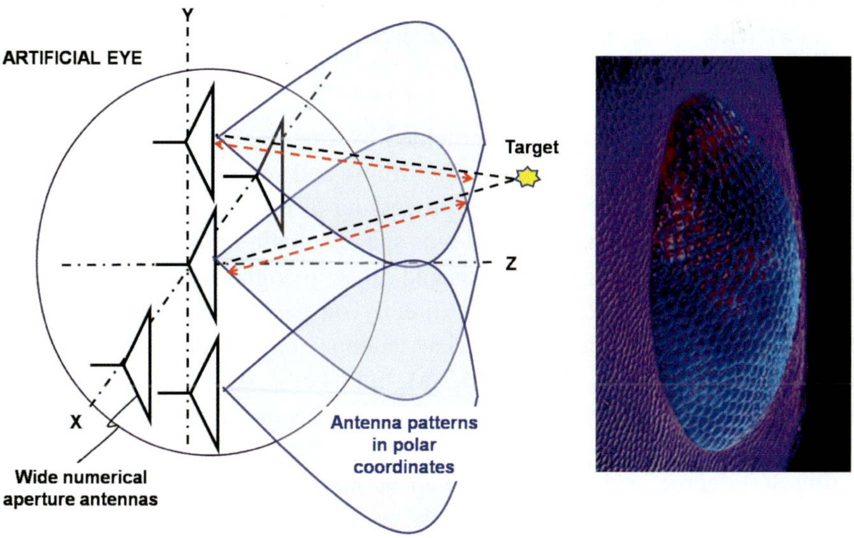

Figure 5.5 Monopulse multi-channel signal processing provides high imaging resolution and fast real-time signal processing. Reference signals provide additional information for the suppression of interference and noise signals.

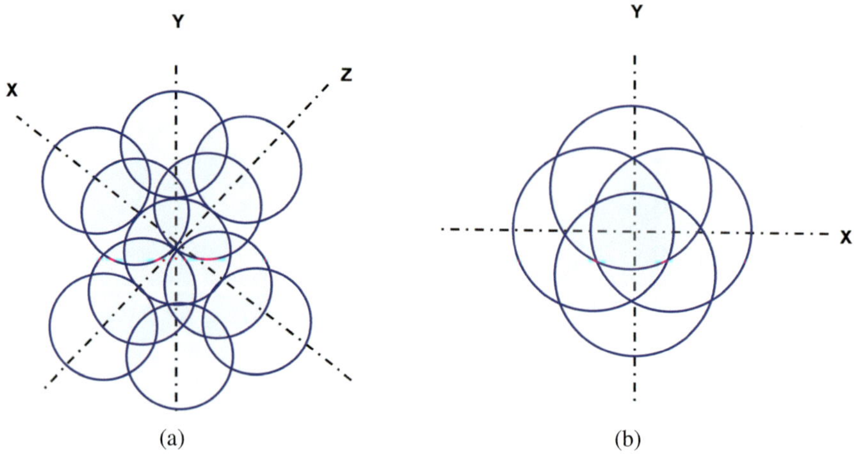

Figure 5.6 Distribution of antenna patterns by three axes (a) and two axes (b) inside the artificial eye.

Fly eye RF radar is integration of a holographic simultaneous wide covering non-scanning system with monopulse high directional accuracy method of multi-beam multi-axis fast signals processing. Radar systems with multi-beam multi-axis overlap antenna patterns with staring, not scanning continuous wide covering area allow receiving maximum non-interrupting information from object or multiple objects. Multi-axis 3D object observation (Figure 5.6) provides high-resolution and high-probability object recognition. High-speed object imaging is provided by simultaneous multi-channel signal processing with fast one-step algorithms and reference signals from overlap antennas. Transformation and processing of received signals in time domain, frequency domain, and multi-axis space domain provides additional possibility to enhance image resolution and object recognition.

Direct digitizing reflected signals directly on each directional antenna allows the distribution of all-around view antennas around the human body on the belt level, as shown in Figure 5.7(a). In this case, directional antennas with overlap antenna patterns will cover 360 degrees in horizontal level and wide, approximately 160 degrees area by elevation. Rings with antenna arrays covering 360-degree horizontal levels can be installed on a few levels. For example, on lower, ground sensing levels, and higher, head sensing levels, as shown in Figure 5.7(b), or even on three levels, including middle, and belt levels, as shown in Figure 5.7 (c). It depends upon the visual system application, which means special function requirements.

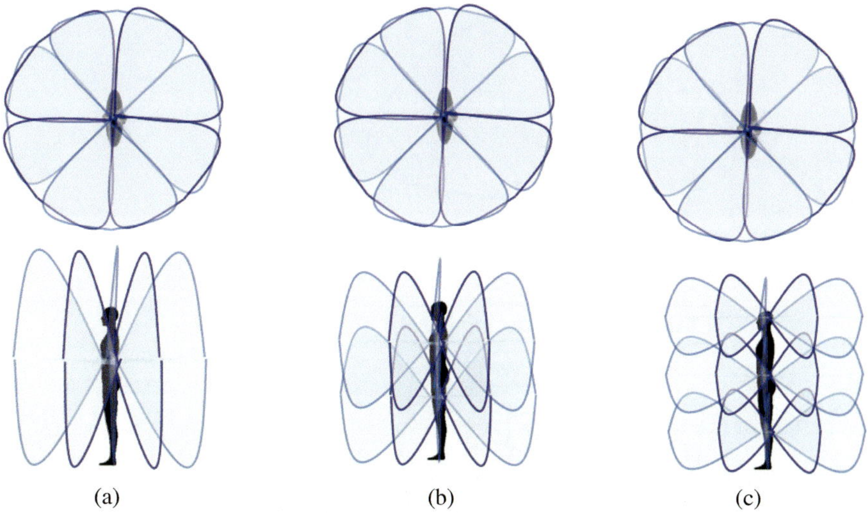

Figure 5.7 Positioning of all-around view antenna arrays on one, two, and three levels relative to the human body, depending on application and function requirements.

The concept of an artificial human vision RF system is presented in Figure 5.8. Transceiver antenna modules (TAM) are positioned on a support ring to form an all-round antenna array covering 360 degrees horizontal level. Direct antenna detection and digitizing of received signals relative to processor time allows simultaneous receiving and registration of amplitudes, phases, and angular distribution of scattered and diffracted spectrum components of all objects around [16–19].

Digital interface allows recording real-time digital holograms in the processor by superposition of scattered and diffracted components regarding the reference time of the transmitted signal. Fourier transform allows the creation of spectrum signatures of detected signals for recognition around objects. Received information is processed to form matching with brain signals and transmitted wirelessly to corresponding brain sections.

5.3 Advances in RF Human Vision System

The accuracy of measuring the range and direction of arrival (DOA) of reflected radiation is crucial for human vision systems. Accuracy estimation involves retrieving the direction information of electromagnetic waves based on the outputs of an antenna array composed of multiple

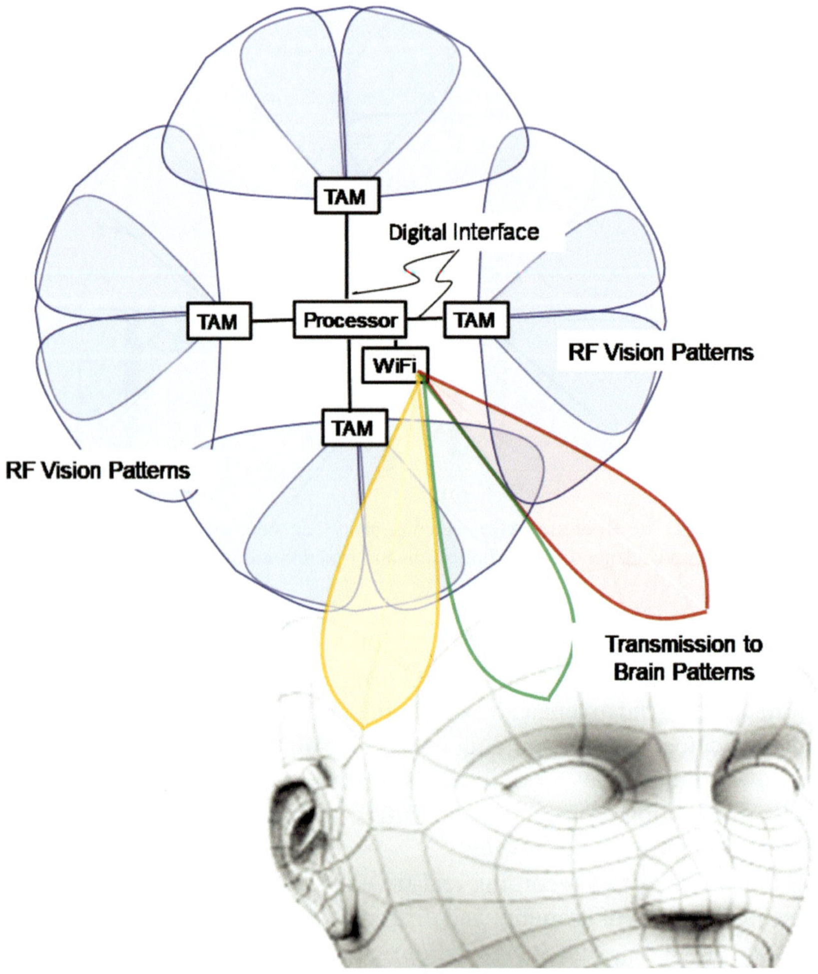

Figure 5.8 Artificial human vision RF system concept that can be installed on the human head and does not require any implants or surgery on brain or eye retinas. The system will provide a 360-degree all-around view and wireless connection with the human brain.

receiving/transmitting antennas. Directional accuracy represents the direction from which a propagating wave arrives at a specific point where the antenna array is located. The measurement of directional accuracy for continuous wave (CW) systems is typically based on the measurement of phase differences between two antennas positioned at a baseline distance in a direction perpendicular to the signal arrival. In the monopulse method of direction finding [13] the use of overlap antenna patterns significantly enhances the accuracy of phase measurements, leading to improved directional accuracy. By employing overlapping antenna patterns, the monopulse system achieves a better resolution in measuring phase differences, resulting in a more precise determination of the direction of the incoming signal or target reflection.

The digitizing of angular distribution patterns of scattered and diffracted frequency components by using the digital holographic matrix, as shown above in Chapter 2, in the combination of the monopulse method allows for a dramatic increase in the phase measurement accuracy, which directly translates into improved directional accuracy in determining the around objects as shown in Figures 5.9–5.10.

High-accuracy phase measurements provide high-accuracy imaging of the human vision system. If antenna lobes are overlapping or closely spaced, a monopulse antenna array can produce a high degree of pointing accuracy within the beam, adding to the normal accuracy of the space-tilted antennas like in the conical scanning system. Whereas classical conical scanning systems generate pointing accuracy on the order of 0.1°; monopulse radars generally improve this by a factor of 10, and advanced tracking radars like the AN/FPS-16 are accurate to 0.006° [20]. The application of digital

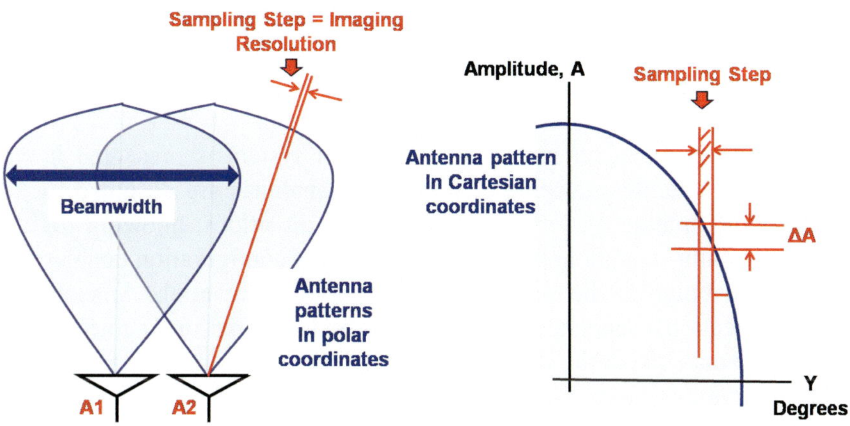

(a) (b)

Figure 5.9 Combination of directional antennas with wide numerical aperture and overlap patterns with direct digitizing of scattered and diffracted receiving frequency components and transfer from time to frequency domain providing theoretically limitless directional accuracy for the human vision system. In contrast to classic radar systems, good penetrating long wavelength RF signals with wide beamwidth practically do not influence system resolution.

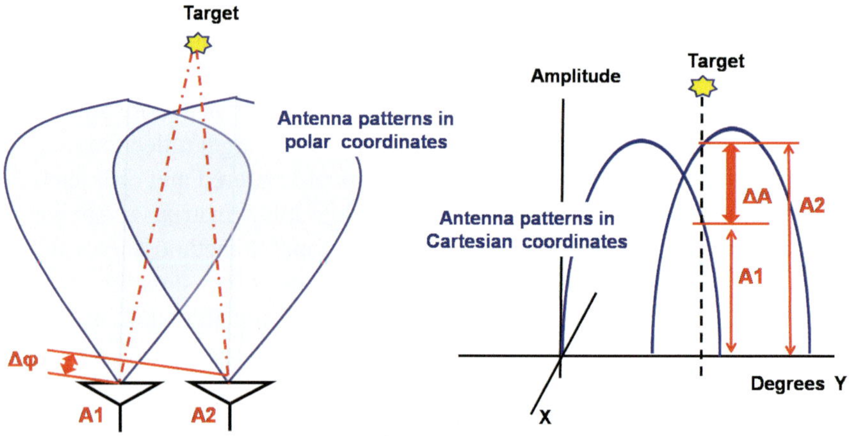

(a) (b)

Figure 5.10 Accuracy of phase measuring can be dramatically enhanced by application of monopulse method by calculation of amplitudes ratio measurement (b) in overlap antenna patterns compared with direct phase difference measurement (a).

holographic method providing better resolution of measurement data 10–100 times and same time can use micro-level human safety low-power RF signals [21].

5.4 Design of Fly Eye Antenna Array for Vision Systems

Nature-inspired design of antenna array for vision system is presented in Figure 5.11. The antenna elements or directional antennas are designed to have overlapping antenna patterns in one or more directions, allowing for the creation of multi-axis monopulse sub-arrays. This configuration enables simultaneous coverage of the entire space or area of observation. Antenna elements or directional antennas may be positioned in some order to form directional antennas inside the dielectric substrate with constant or variable dielectric constant, or as a 3D metamaterial substrate. An antenna array arranged as a plurality of antenna elements can be formed by positioning antenna elements inside and on the surface of the dielectric substrate. Directional antennas also can be arranged inside dielectric material layer attached to main transceiver substrate.

The positioning of receiver antenna modules (RAMs) to form a monopulse sub-array antenna system is presented in Figure 5.12. Four

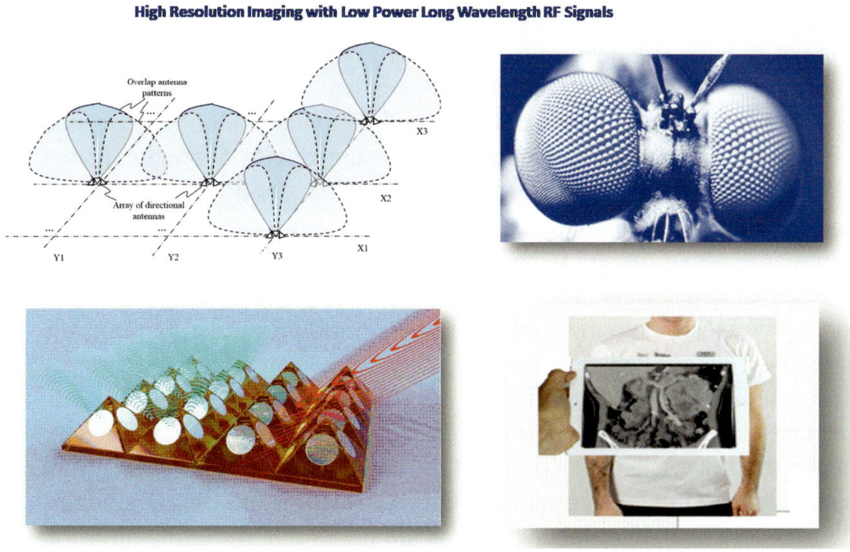

Figure 5.11 Nature-inspired antenna arrays with two-axes positioning of directional antennas can be applied for high-resolution RF portable artificial vision systems for the detection and recognition of concealed objects.

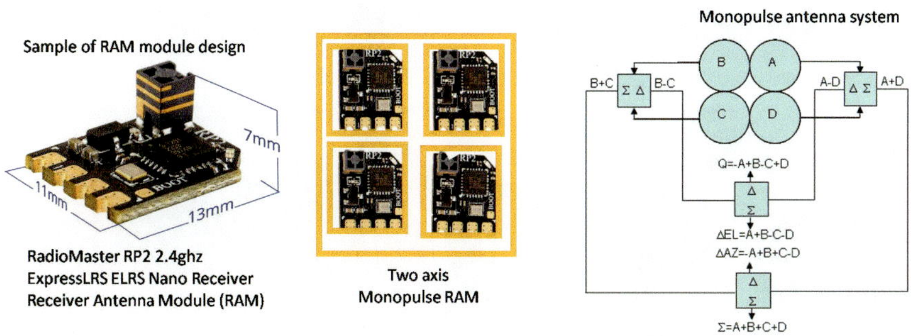

Figure 5.12 Sample of nano receiver antenna module and positioning of four modules for forming monopulse sub-array antenna system.

nano receiver antenna modules comprising helical directional antennas with circular polarization integrated to monopulse sub-array antenna system. RAM is positioned by vertical and horizontal axes to provide vertical and horizontal directions measurement.

The antenna elements can be designed as resonance antennas, suitable for operating at specific frequencies, such as Yagi antennas or helical antennas. Alternatively, non-resonance frequency independent traveling-wave antennas or quantum antennas can be utilized to extend the bandwidth of the antenna array. These traveling-wave antennas can be arranged with discrete radiators placed at specific distances along the axis or in the form of a continuous radiator that extends in the direction of the axis.

Different kinds of directional antenna arrays can be applied for artificial vision systems. Directional antennas can be circularly polarized or have one, two, or a few axes of polarization, be shielded and/or have ground plates. Arrays can be distributed on spherical, convex, concave, flat surfaces, or closely located, as presented in Figure 5.13.

Antennas can be designed for one frequency, or have wide bandwidth, depending on the application. Two or four antennas can be integrated into the monopulse module, which includes direct detection and digitizing chips (Figure 5.14). Helical directional antennae are preferable for artificial vision systems where the polarization of received signals may be different. One or two axes polarization antennas are usually used for systems, where the polarization of transmitting/receiving signals are determined and known.

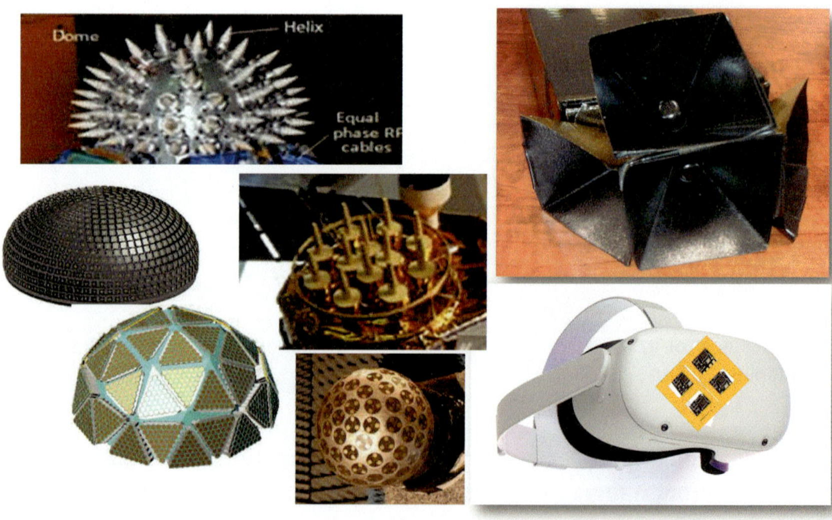

Figure 5.13 Samples of different kinds of antenna arrays with directional antennas designed for different applications.

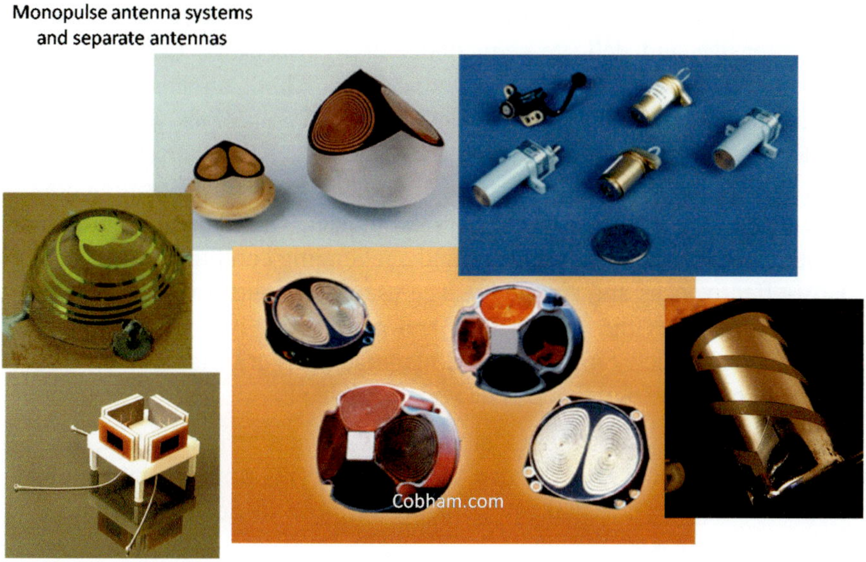

Figure 5.14 Directional nano-antenna and wide bandwidth antennas integrated into monopulse modules with direct detection and digitizing chips.

Conclusion

Advantages over traditional human vision:

- Extended EM wave frequency range. Unlike the natural human eye, which is limited to the visible spectrum, the artificial vision system can extend the range of detectable electromagnetic (EM) waves. This allows for the perception of a broader spectrum, including infrared and ultraviolet light, thus providing enhanced situational awareness and capabilities.
- Extended range and field of view. The artificial vision system can be designed to extend both the range and field of view beyond natural human capabilities. This includes the ability to see distant objects more clearly and to have a wider field of view, which is beneficial in various applications such as surveillance, navigation, and exploration.
- Vision of concealed objects. The system can penetrate through obstructions like walls or the ground, using RF waves to detect and visualize concealed objects. This capability is particularly useful in search and rescue operations, security, and medical diagnostics.

- Possibility to use of simple metal RF antenna arrays. Instead of relying on expensive and delicate semiconductor light sensors, the proposed system utilizes simple metal RF antenna arrays. These antennas are more robust and reliable under various environmental conditions, making the system more durable and cost-effective. The metal RF antenna arrays are less susceptible to damage from environmental factors such as temperature fluctuations, humidity, and physical impact. This reliability ensures consistent performance in diverse and challenging conditions.
- Cost-effectiveness and simplicity. The use of straightforward metal RF antennas reduces the overall cost and complexity of the vision system. This simplicity in design and manufacturing translates to a more accessible technology that can be widely adopted.

The artificial eye can serve as an advanced human vision system, augmenting natural sight with extended capabilities. This could significantly benefit individuals with visual impairments or those in need of enhanced vision for specific tasks.

The vision system can be integrated into various technical systems, such as autonomous vehicles, drones, and robotics, enhancing their ability to navigate and interact with their environment.

In medical fields, the system can be used for non-invasive diagnostics, allowing for the detection of abnormalities beneath the skin or within the body without the need for invasive procedures.

The extended range and field of view, along with the ability to see concealed objects, make the system ideal for security and surveillance applications, providing comprehensive monitoring capabilities.

In industrial settings, the vision system can be used for quality control, inspection, and monitoring, ensuring high standards and efficiency in manufacturing processes.

The proposed nature-inspired vision system represents a significant advancement in imaging technology. By combining limitless controllable resolution, extended EM wave detection, and robust, cost-effective RF antenna arrays, the system offers numerous benefits over traditional human vision. Its potential applications span a wide range of fields, promising to enhance both human and technical capabilities without the need for invasive procedures or expensive components. This innovative approach paves the way for a new era of artificial vision technology.

References

[1] Automated Imaging Association (AIA), [Online]. Available www.visiononline.org , https://en.wikipedia.org/wiki/Automated_Imaging_Association [Accessed April 20, 2024].

[2] Neurolink Inc. [Online]Available www.neuralink.com [Accessed April 20, 2024].

[3] Cortigent inc. [Online] Available www.cortigent.com [Accessed April 20, 2024]. UT Southwestern Medical Center, [Onlne] Available https://utswmed.org/doctors/nader-pouratian , https://utswmed.org [Accessed April 20, 2023].

[4] LiveScience, Bionic eye, [Online] https://www.livescience.com/bionic-eye [Accessed April 20, 2023].

[5] Stanford Medicine, Chichilnisky Lab, Chichilnisky Lab | Chichilnisky Lab | Stanford Medicine. 2024.

[6] The Argus(®) II Retinal Prosthesis System – PubMed, [Online] Available https://pubmed.ncbi.nlm.nih.gov/26404104 [Accessed Apil 20, 2024].

[7] Pixium Vision Inc. France, [Online] Available www.pixium-vision.com [Accessed April 20, 2024].

[8] NanoRetina Inc. Israel, [Online] Available www.nano-retina.com [Accessed April 20, 2024].

[9] P. A. Molchanov, "Seeing Invisible: Advanced Antenna Arrays," River Publishers, February 2024. ISBN: 9781003476559, [Online] Available www.riverpublishers.com marketing@riverpublishers.com Accessed April 20, 2024].

[10] P. Molchanov, "Multi-Antenna Array for All Space Communications," 2024 IEEE Radio Wireless Week (RWW), San Antonio, TX, USA, January 21, 2024.

[11] S. A. Harman "A comparison of staring radars with scanning radars for UAV detection: introduction of the Alarm TM staring radar," 2015, European Radar Conference (EURAD), 185-188, XP032824534, EUMA, Sep. 2015.

[12] S. A. Harman, "Holographic Radar Development," (Aveillant Ltd., Cambridge, U.K.)," 2021-02-07, [Online] Available www.microwavejournal.com [Accessed April 20, 2023].

[13] S. E. Lipsky, "Microwave Passive Direction Finder," SciTech Publishing Inc. Raleigh, NC 27613, 2004.

[14] L. Zhena, B. Decang, C. Weibiao, L. Jiqiaoa , Z. Xiaopeng, "Antenna efficiency and aperture optimization analysis of spaceborne coherent wind lidar," (SAME2023), Proc. of SPIE Vol.12706, 127060E © 2023 SPIE. 2023.

[15] N. Chantier, J. Cochard, "Software-defined direct RF simultaneous sampling multi-band/service transceiver," Teledyne e2v Semiconductors, France, MWJOURNAL.COM, DECEMBER 2022, p. 22-42.

[16] S. Lischi, R. Massini, R. Pilard, D. Stagliano and N. Chantier, "Feasibility study of a fully-digital multi-band SAR system operating at L, C, X and Ku Bands," 7th Workshop on RF and Microwave Systems, Instruments & Sub-systems, 5th Ka-band Workshop, May 2022.

[17] F. Deviere, N. Seller and J. Rohou, "Making history: advanced system in a package technology enable direct RF conversion," White paper, Microwave Journal, Vol. 64, No. 1, January 2021.

[18] T. O'Farrell, R. Singh, Q. Bai, K. L. Ford, R. Langley, M. Beach, E. Arabi, C. Gamlath and K. A. Morris, "Tunable, concurrent multi-band, single chain radio architecture for low energy 5G-Rans," IEEE 85th Vehicular Technology Conference (VTC Spring), June 2017.

[19] Wikipedia, Monopulse radar, [Online] Available www.wikipedia.com [Accessed April 20, 2024].

[20] P. Molchanov, "Objects Recognition in High-scattering Conditions at Radio/Microwave Frequency," SPIE Defense + Commercial Sensing conference, National Harbor, Washington DC, April, 2024.

6

Artificial Intelligence in Vision Systems: AI Fabric

Introduction

Artificial Intelligence (AI) Fabric in a vision system is a unified platform designed to integrate digital holographic data with Fresnel coherent diffraction imaging (FCDI) analytics tools. This combination creates a novel AI-involved technology capable of achieving human-like scalability in vision resolution and recognition without relying on precise lenses or moving mechanical parts. This platform addresses challenges in vision resolution by applying digital holographic processing methods to signals captured by nature-inspired wide numerical aperture sensor arrays. It achieves this by converting the diffraction limit from spatial pixel size to the time/frequency domain, allowing for scalable sampling and digitizing frequencies to measure diffracted signal components. Additionally, direct digital coherent processing of diffracted frequency components and angular spectral pattern analysis enables high-resolution, non-invasive remote detection and recognition of objects or anomalies in high-scattering mediums based on spectrum signatures.

6.1 Artificial Intelligence in Vision Systems

The design of artificial vision represents a departure from traditional image processing technology, instead of focusing on imaging technology that utilizes electromagnetic signals for recognizing and imaging small objects across varying distances, including those hidden or buried underground. This approach leverages long-wavelength radio frequency radar to generate high-resolution images. The proposed imaging radar system operates by processing wavefront signals reflected from objects, which are recorded as digital holograms. It employs a staring (non-scanning, non-switching) antenna array capable of covering the entire object simultaneously. By synchronizing with processor time, this system achieves efficient data processing. Monopulse processing of antenna signals, combined with overlapping antenna patterns, enhances directional resolution. Furthermore, the distribution of overlap antennas across multiple axes and the incorporation of reference antennas maximize the information available about the shape and dielectric properties of the object being imaged.

The Fresnel coherent diffraction imaging (FCDI) analytics tool represents a groundbreaking technology offering the potential for electronically scalable control of imaging resolution and recognition, without the need for precise lenses or moving mechanical parts. Figure 6.1 illustrates the signal processing algorithm and image generation in an artificial RF imaging system. The signal processing can be segmented into three main parts.

Firstly, it involves the transmission of electromagnetic signals and the reception of scattered and diffracted patterns containing comprehensive information about the objects and the scattering medium. Secondly, monopulse signal processing is utilized for receiving range and positioning information, enhancing the accuracy of the imaging system. Finally, the third part involves the recording of a holographic database, which is subsequently

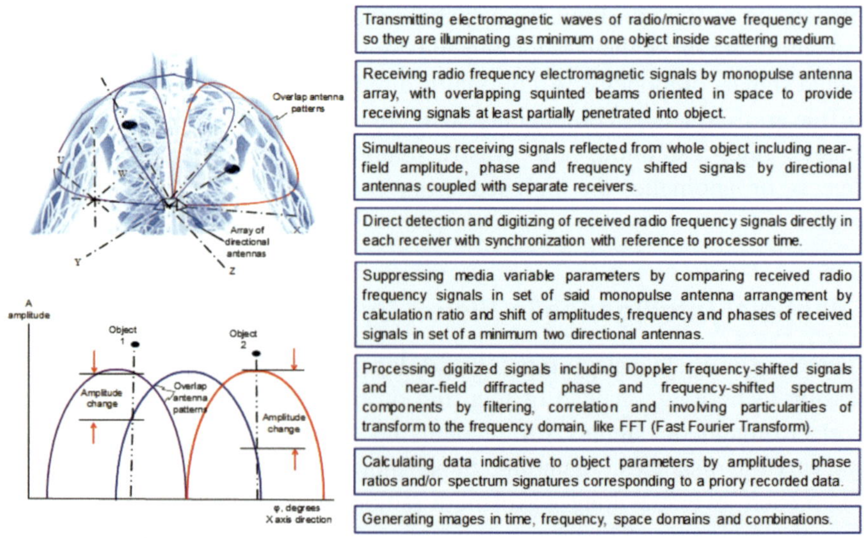

Figure 6.1 Block diagram representing algorithm of signal processing and image generation in artificial RF medical imaging system.

employed for imaging and object recognition purposes. This comprehensive approach enables the system to capture, process, and utilize data efficiently for high-resolution imaging and accurate object recognition.

Automatic signal processing within the RF imaging system can be divided into three primary blocks (Figure 6.2).

The first block, TAM (transceiver antenna module), encompasses the functions of transmitting, receiving, and preliminary conditioning of signals reflected from objects.

The second block, MSP (multi-channel monopulse signal processor), is responsible for direct detection, digitizing, and monopulse signal processing.

Finally, the third block, HOB (holographic database), serves as a real-time recording database, responsible for the calculation of object parameters and the generation of images.

These three blocks collectively form a robotic automation platform (RPA), which serves as a centralized repository for structured and semi-structured data. This database allows for access to data visualization and various forms of intelligence reporting [1–5].

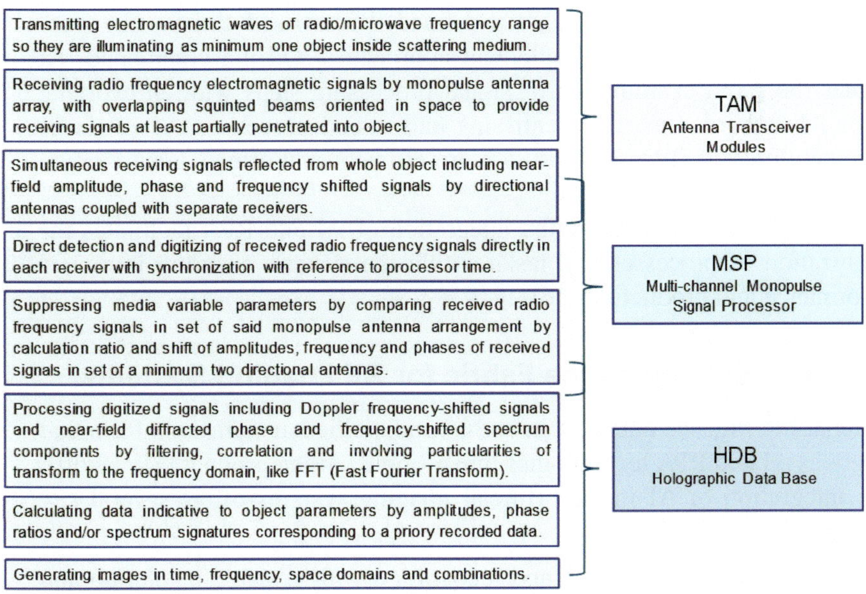

Figure 6.2 Automatic signal processing can be divided into three blocks, TAM, MSP, and HOB.

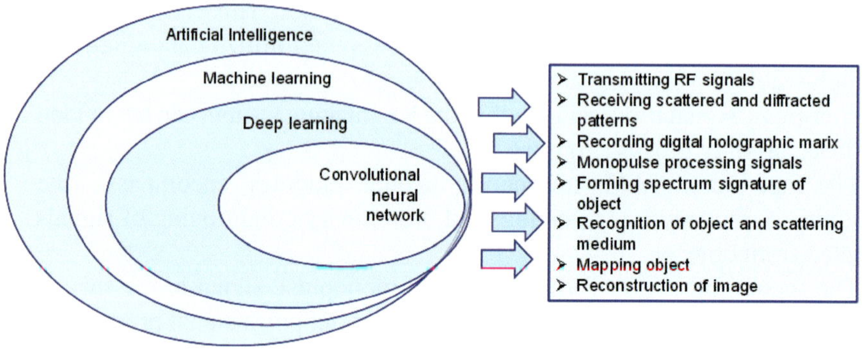

Figure 6.3 Relation of AI platform and signal processing steps in RF artificial imaging system.

The integration of robotic process automation (RPA) and artificial intelligence (AI) provides a centralized platform for developing, deploying, and managing AI models within the system. This combination leverages the strengths of both technologies to solve a broad range of tasks while ensuring control over imaging accuracy and efficiency.

RPA excels at automating well-defined, rules-based tasks using simple algorithms and easy-to-implement approaches. On the other hand, AI enables the rapid examination of signal processing steps with an evolving set of AI technologies. By identifying end-to-end processes, AI enhances the capabilities of RPA, leading to more efficient and effective automation solutions.

Figure 6.3 illustrates how the integration of AI and RPA facilitates the optimization of processes and tasks within the system, ensuring improved performance and productivity [6].

6.2 Artificial Intelligence Fabric for RF Imaging Systems

Artificial Intelligence Fabric is an end-to-end, unified analytics platform that integrates AI and RPA technologies into a single unified product [Microsoft]. This integration of AI in RF artificial imaging systems offers several key functions:

- Automatic image display and recognition with scalable resolution and human-like accuracy.
- Extraction of critical information from a holographic database for display.

► Instant resolution of remote real-time service requests.

By providing integration of RPA and AI technologies, the Artificial Intelligence Fabric represents a significant advancement in intelligent automation (Figure 6.4). In a multi-channel RF imaging system, RPA manages sensor modules and processes sensor signals to create a holographic database. Directional antennas form an array with overlap patterns and serve as sensors for the RF system's frequency range. AI analytics tools, including data services, machine learning, and neural network tools, facilitate model training and storage of processed data. RPA and AI operate as separate processes, but their integration through AI Fabric creates a symbiotic relationship. This integration breaks down barriers, seamlessly combining RPA's implementation with AI's cognitive power:

► A common interface allows for deploying AI models into an RPA workflow.
► AI handles model training, rewriting, and development.
► AI integration provides end-to-end visibility of model versioning and updates.
► Advanced model management and monitoring are enabled through AI performance analysis.

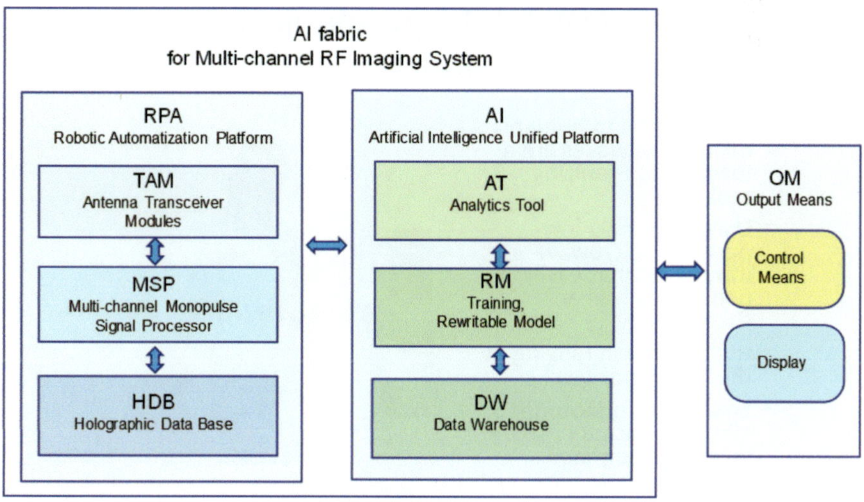

Figure 6.4 AI fabric for multi-channel RF imaging system integrating robotic automatization platform with artificial intelligence unified platform and providing unification of output signals for display and control.

- The data feedback loop ensures continuous improvement of AI models over time.

Output means typically include some form of display and control mechanisms. These output means can be wirelessly connected to a multi-channel RF imaging system through a digital interface. This interface facilitates two-way communication, allowing for the reception of imaging information and the control of the imaging system.

6.3 Artificial RF Vision Systems for Medical Imaging

Remote radar imaging systems are used for different medical and biomedical applications. The main advance of RF signals is good penetration into human body, which allows to use very small power safety for human radio signals (Figure 6.5).

RF digital holographic system was tested for remote human body imaging, breathing or heart motion detection, and tissue recognition (Figure 6.6). Measured directional and lateral resolution of the system was 100 times smaller than the applied wavelength as shown in Chapter 2. Human breathing and heart motions were detected through 30 inches of concrete wall, as shown

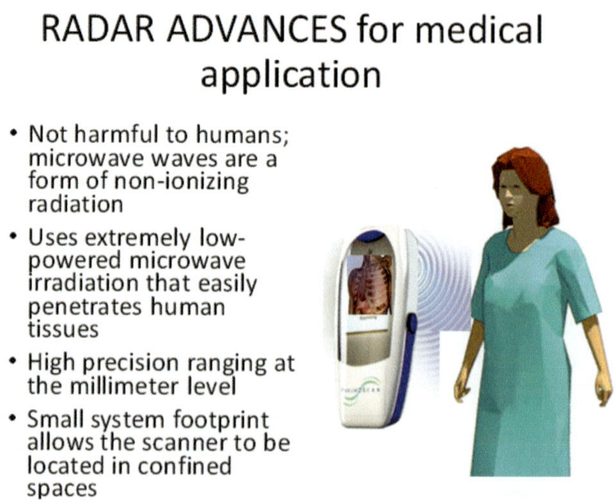

Figure 6.5 Radar advances for medical applications including using safety for human micro-level of radio signals and simple commercially available low-profile inexpensive elements. Same time RF digital holographic imaging systems can provide high-resolution human-like vision.

in Chapter 4. The results of remote object recognition were presented in Chapter 3.

The diagram in Figure 6.7 presents the application of CW RF signal for recording of coherent diffraction patterns reflected from some object or anomaly inside the human body.

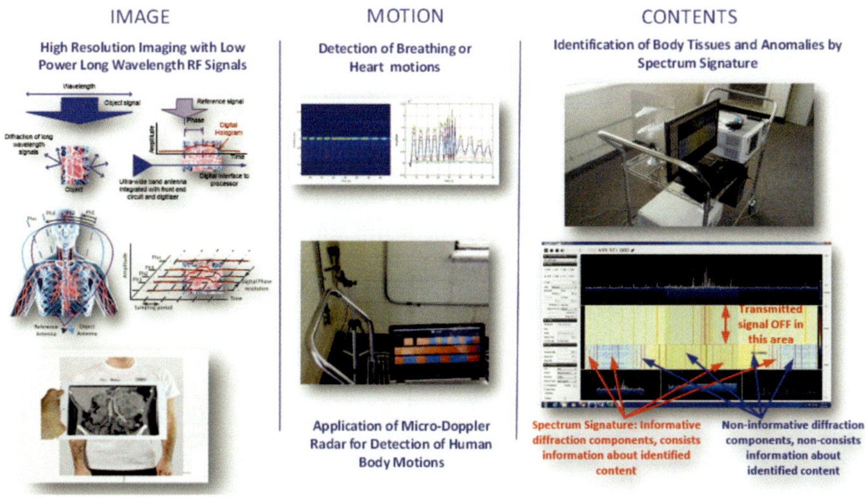

Figure 6.6 Remote RF digital holographic system can provide inside human body imaging, detection of motion, including detection of breathing and heart motions, and recognition of body tissues or anomalies in different parts inside the human body.

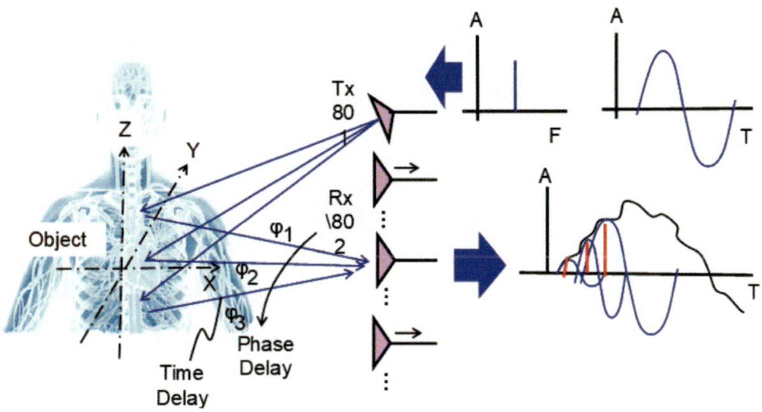

Figure 6.7 Transmitting of CW RF sinusoidal signal and recording of scattered and diffracted inside human body patterns with wide numerical aperture sensors and digital holography.

The wavelength of RF transmitted CW signal is usually relatively larger than imaging objects and we will talk about scattered and diffracted by object frequency components. Signals scattered and diffracted by an object or part of the object and received by a wide numerical aperture sensor will be superpositioned regarding the transmitted signal. Real-time Fourier transform of received signals from time to frequency domain will allow filtering scattered and diffracted frequency components and form spectrum signature of object (Figure 6.8).

Spectrum signatures of different objects can be divided to groups comprising lot of different information of object. It may be information about the shape, size, and dielectric properties of object. Remote RF digital holographic system was tested for measurement spectrum signatures of glucose dissolved in water and is presented in Figure 6.9. Spectrum signature allows to separate

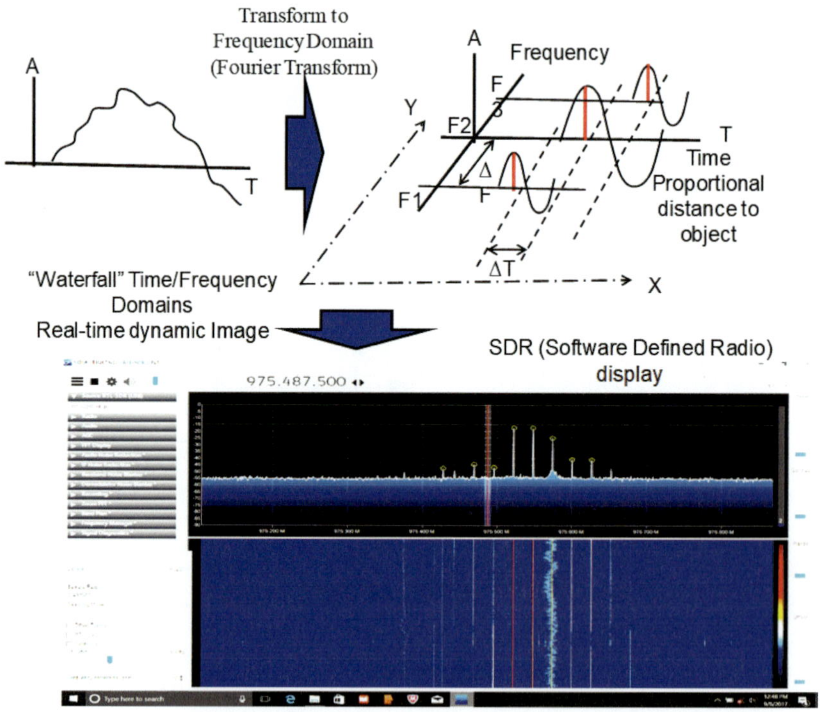

Figure 6.8 SDR is transferring received by wide aperture sensor frequency components to the frequency domain and forming of spectrum signature of the object on display. Real-time change of spectrum signature or "waterfall" also allows observation of change of spectrum signatures in time and Doppler shifts.

frequency components corresponding to water or background, and components corresponding to concentration of dissolved glucose. Components corresponding to dissolved glucose can be shifted, increased, or decreased depending on glucose concentration.

The visualization of objects or anomalies remotely detected inside the human body by Fresnel coherent diffracting visual system is provided by inverse Fourier transform of received scattered and diffracted frequency components to the two or three axes time domain coordinates as presented in Figure 6.10.

Block diagram of multi-channel RF artificial medical imaging and identification system with ultrasound focusing on the limited area of observation is presented in Figure 6.11. The system comprises an antenna array with reference antenna, TAM (transceiver antenna module) comprising software-defined radio (SDR) for transmitting, receiving, and digitizing signals coupled with a monopulse signal processor to form a holographic matrix. Artificial intelligence block comprises an analytic tool for training models and image generator. Antenna array arranged as an array of directional antennas covering a wide area of observation with staring, not scanning, overlap in as minimum one axis antenna patterns creating antenna sub-arrays

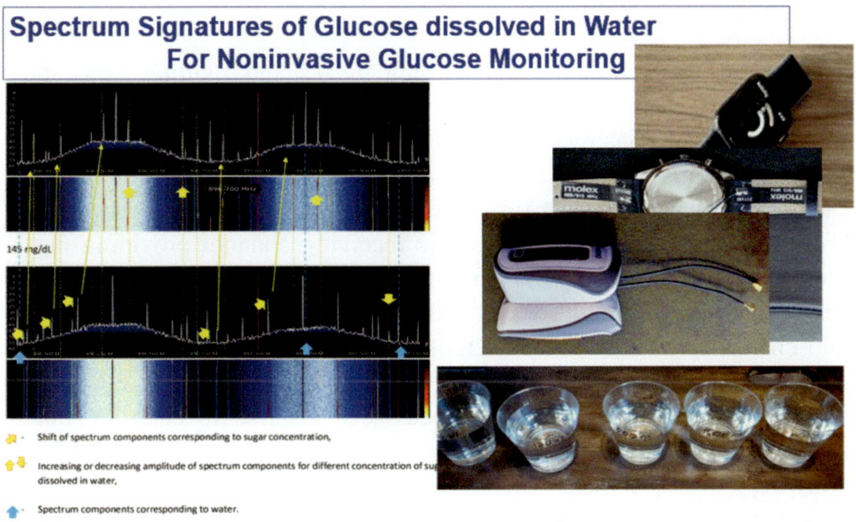

Figure 6.9 Spectrum signatures of glucose dissolved in water with change of glucose concentration. Test made with different glucose concentrations and with different sensors/antenna constructions.

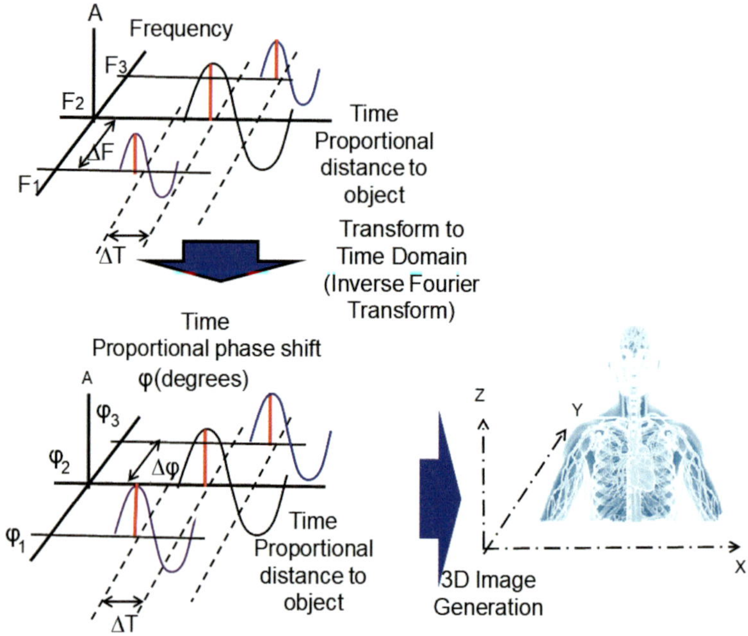

Figure 6.10 Reconstruction of object image by inverse Fourier transform of scattered and diffracted frequency components to the time domain in two or three axes coordinates.

in each axis. SDR comprising transmitting means and multiple separate receiving channels with signal conditioning circuits including voltage and/or current limiters, anti-aliasing circuits, automatic gain control (AGC) means, directional coupler with signal detector and analog-to-digital converter.

Each directional antenna covers whole area or a sub-sector of the area of observation and coupled with separate receiving channel providing fast continuous parallel processing of signals for receiving maximum information from all covering areas simultaneously. Monopulse signal processor arranged as multi-channel processor is connected with an image generator and comprising memory for real-time recording digital hologram, synchronization means and at least one monopulse processor connected to each antenna sub-array by directional coupler with signal detector for creating monopulse sub-arrays.

Monopulse sub-arrays comprising means for one or multi-axis processing of all signals in receiving channels as ratio of amplitudes and/or phase shift of signals for direction finding and one-iteration adapting for clutter suppressing or decrease transferring scattering medium influence to receiving chain

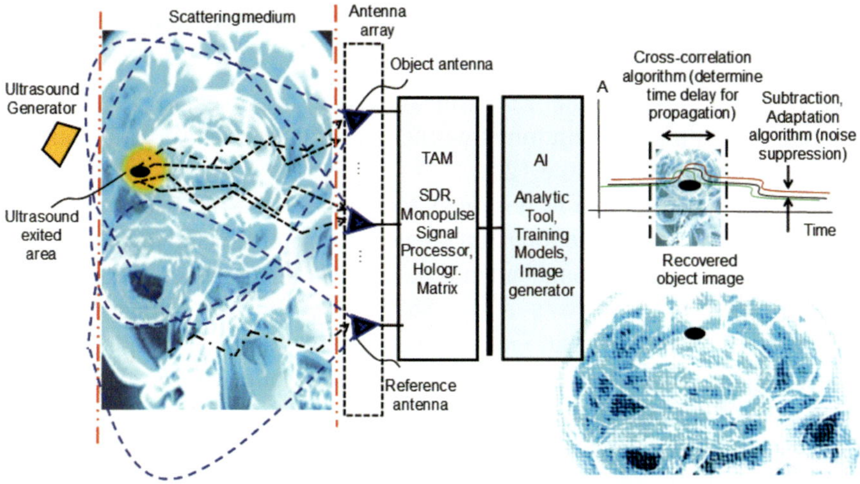

Figure 6.11 RF artificial medical imaging system with ultrasound focusing on the limited area of observation.

parameters by a phase shift in sub-array of neighboring directional antennas with overlap antenna patterns, wherein application of signals from reference antennas providing highest directional accuracy and better clutter/noise and media influence suppression.

The multi-channel processor also comprised means for transforming, correcting, and filter received signals from the time domain to the frequency domain and space one axis and/or multi-axis domain to increase image resolution and number of parameters for object recognition. The cross-correlation algorithm allows adjusting and determines time delay for propagation. Subtraction and adaptation algorithm provides noise suppression. Focused ultrasound exited area allows to limited area of observation for more accurate imaging of object position. Antenna array, receiving, and processing means arranged for receiving additional Doppler shifted by ultrasound and diffracted spectrum components in the near field consists of information about objects limited by ultrasound excited area, objects content by spectrum signature, and object shape. Said image generator is arranged for generating one or multi-axis images in time, frequency, space, or combined domains. SDR with monopulse processor, image generator, and ultrasound signal generator are connected by digital interface arranged as universal serial bus (USB) or microwave and/or fiber optic waveguides to signal processor or wireless (not shown).

6.3.1 RF artificial medical imaging system with ultrasound focusing

Block diagram of multi-channel RF artificial medical imaging and identification system with ultrasound illuminating the slice of area of observation and imaging is presented in Figure 6.12.

The system architecture is designed for high-resolution imaging and object recognition using directional antennas and a sophisticated signal processing chain. Each directional antenna is configured to cover the entire observation area or sub-sectors of it. These antennas are coupled with separate receiving channels that facilitate fast, continuous, and parallel processing of signals. This setup ensures the maximum amount of information is captured from all areas simultaneously.

The system comprising at least one TAM (transceiver antenna module) comprising as minimum one object antenna and as minimum one reference antenna, software defined radio (SDR) for transmitting, receiving and digitizing signals coupled with monopulse signal processor and means for real-time recording holographic matrix. Said antenna array arranged as array of directional antennas covering wide area of observation with staring, not scanning, overlap in as minimum one axis antenna patterns creating antenna sub-arrays in each axis. SDR comprises transmitting means and multiple separate receiving channels with signal conditioning circuits including voltage or

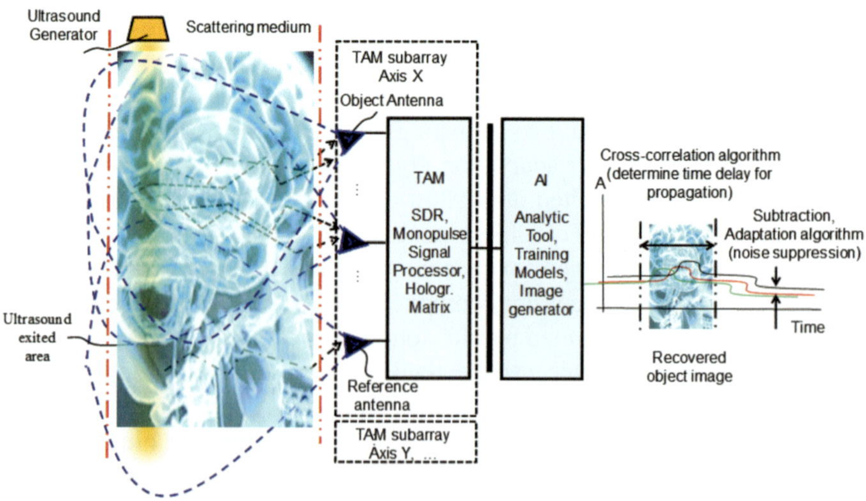

Figure 6.12 Block diagram of multi-channel RF artificial medical imaging and identification system with ultrasound illuminating the slice of the area of observation and imaging.

current limiters, anti-aliasing circuits, AGC means, directional coupler with signal detector and analog-to-digital converter. Each directional antenna covers whole area or a sub-sector of the area of observation coupled with separate receiving channel providing fast continuous parallel processing of signals for receiving maximum information from all covering area simultaneously [7–11].

This advanced system architecture leverages a combination of directional antennas, monopulse signal processing, and sophisticated algorithms to deliver high-resolution imaging and precise object recognition. The integration of ultrasound for focused observation areas further enhances the system's capabilities, making it suitable for a wide range of applications in challenging environments. The use of SDR and digital holography ensures flexibility, scalability, and real-time processing, positioning this technology at the forefront of imaging and recognition systems.

The proposed artificial RF vision system with digital holography and focused ultrasound presents a novel approach to medical imaging. This system allows for high-resolution, non-invasive imaging, and detection of various conditions within the human body, providing a significant advancement over traditional imaging methods.

Conclusion

The Artificial Intelligence (AI) Fabric in a vision system that represents a significant advancement in imaging technology, offering a unified platform that integrates digital holographic data with Fresnel coherent diffraction imaging (FCDI) analytics tools. This innovative combination leads to the development of AI-involved technology capable of achieving human-like scalability in vision resolution and recognition without the need for precise lenses or moving mechanical parts.

The AI Fabric addresses challenges in vision resolution by utilizing digital holographic processing methods. Signals captured by nature-inspired wide numerical aperture sensor arrays are processed by converting the diffraction limit from spatial pixel size to the time/frequency domain. This approach allows for scalable sampling and digitizing frequencies, enabling precise measurement of diffracted signal components.

By employing direct digital coherent processing of diffracted frequency components and angular spectral pattern analysis, the system achieves high-resolution, non-invasive remote detection, and recognition of objects or anomalies. This capability is particularly effective in high-scattering mediums, where traditional imaging methods struggle.

The system leverages spectrum signatures for object recognition. The Fourier transform and filtering of diffracted components allow for the separation of objects from the surrounding medium, providing valuable information about an object's dielectric properties, size, and shape, which remain invariant to the object's spatial position.

The use of long-wavelength radio frequency signals enhances the system's ability to penetrate various materials, making it suitable for applications requiring non-invasive remote sensing. This is especially beneficial in medical imaging, environmental monitoring, and security applications.

The technology mimics human vision by offering electronic control over focus, field of view (FOV), direction, and resolution. This flexibility allows the system to adapt to different imaging requirements dynamically.

The system's ability to function across various electromagnetic spectra (RF, microwave, IR, UV, X-ray, and gamma-ray) makes it versatile for applications ranging from interferometric microscopy to health monitoring and tactical optic/microwave systems.

The integration of AI with digital holographic processing and FCDI analytics tools marks a transformative approach to vision systems. This platform not only enhances imaging resolution and recognition accuracy but also introduces new possibilities for non-invasive diagnostics and monitoring in challenging environments. The technology's adaptability and scalability suggest a broad potential for future developments in both human and technical vision applications.

The proposed AI fabric in vision systems represents a groundbreaking step forward in imaging technology. Its ability to achieve high-resolution, non-invasive detection and recognition in high-scattering mediums, combined with human-like scalability in vision resolution and control, opens new avenues for innovation and application across diverse fields.

References

[1] Introducing Microsoft Fabric: The data platform for the era of AI, Microsoft Azure Blog, [Online], Available Introducing Microsoft Fabric: The data platform for the era of AI | Microsoft Azure Blog | Microsoft Azure [Accessed April 12, 2024].

[2] AI Center - AI Fabric architecture, [Online], Available www.uipath.com [Accessed April 12, 2024].

[3] The first AI model based on Yann LeCun's vision for more human-like AI, [Olnine] Available www.meta.com [Accessed April12, 2024].
[4] Computer Vision in AI (Artificial Intelligence), [Online] Available www.almabetter.com [Accessed April 12, 2024].
[5] New Technology Gives AI Human-Like Eyes, [Online], Available https: //scitechdaily.com [Accessed Aplil 12, 2024].
[6] Basic CNN Architecture: "Explaining 5 Layers of Convolutional Neural Network US," [Online] Available https://staging-mp.uupgrad.dev/blog/basic-cnn-architecture-explaining-5-layers-of-convolutional-neural-network-us/ [Accessed April 12, 2024].
[7] N. Chantier, J. Cochard, "Software-defined direct RF simultaneous sampling multi-band/service transceiver," Teledyne e2v Semiconductors, France, MWJOURNAL.COM, DECEMBER 2022, p. 22-42.
[8] S. Lischi, R. Massini, R. Pilard, D. Stagliano and N. Chantier, "Feasibility study of a fully-digital multi-band SAR system operating at L, C, X and Ku Bands," 7th Workshop on RF and Microwave Systems, Instruments & Sub-systems, 5th Ka-band Workshop, May 2022.
[9] F. Deviere, N. Seller and J. Rohou, "Making history: advanced system in a package technology enable direct RF conversion," White paper, Microwave Journal, Vol. 64, No. 1, January 2021.
[10] T. O'Farrell, R. Singh, Q. Bai, K. L. Ford, R. Langley, M. Beach, E. Arabi, C. Gamlath and K. A. Morris, "Tunable, concurrent multi-band, single chain radio architecture for low energy 5G-Rans," IEEE 85th Vehicular Technology Conference (VTC Spring), June 2017.
[11] P. Molchanov, "Objects Recognition in High-scattering Conditions at Radio/Microwave Frequency," SPIE Defense + Commercial Sensing conference, National Harbor, Washington DC, April, 2024.
[12] Y. Zhang, Y. Wu, C. Huang, Z.-W. Zhou, M. Li, Z. Zhang, J. Chen, "Deep-learning enhanced high-quality imaging in metalens-integrated camera," Opt. Lett., Vol. 49, Issue 10, pp. 2853-2856, 2024.

7

Applications of New High-resolution Vision Technology

Introduction

The novel, nature-inspired high-resolution vision technology is not limited by optical wavelengths but can be applied to imaging and recognizing objects with electromagnetic waves across radio frequency (RF), microwave, IR, UV, X-ray, and gamma-ray spectra in high-scattering mediums. It offers enhanced imaging resolution and object recognition in various domains:

Interferometric microscopy: This technology can significantly improve the resolution of interferometric microscopes, allowing for detailed visualization at the cellular and molecular levels. It facilitates non-invasive imaging techniques that can be used in biomedical research and diagnostics.

Health monitoring: The technology can be used for high-resolution imaging of internal organs and tissues, providing critical insights for medical diagnostics and treatment planning. It enables remote monitoring of patients' health by providing detailed images and data without the need for invasive procedures.

Tactical optic/microwave systems: The technology can be applied in military and security applications for high-resolution surveillance and reconnaissance, detecting concealed objects and threats. It aids in navigation and guidance systems by providing precise imaging and object recognition capabilities in challenging environments.

Remote digital holographic systems: These systems can be used for monitoring environmental conditions and changes, such as pollution levels and natural disasters. They are valuable in industrial applications for inspecting machinery and infrastructure, ensuring safety and reliability.

Astronomical observations: The technology enhances the resolution of telescopes, allowing for more detailed observations of distant celestial objects. It improves adaptive optics systems, compensating for atmospheric distortions and providing clearer images of space.

Communications: The technology can enhance the transmission of signals in communication systems, improving clarity and reducing interference. It facilitates high-speed data transfer over long distances with minimal loss of information.

By integrating these advanced capabilities, the novel vision technology opens up a multitude of possibilities across various fields, driving innovation and improving efficiency in both scientific research and practical applications. Several applications of remote digital holographic systems are presented below in this chapter.

7.1 Water–Air Wireless Communication System

Exploration of the ocean is essential for various critical activities, including environmental monitoring, climate assessment, pollution tracking, oil and gas exploration, natural disaster prediction, resource exploration, deep-sea archaeology, scientific data collection, marine biology, and oceanography. These activities often require advanced techniques and technologies for communication, imaging, and mapping to detect and survey objects in the ocean.

Application of radio frequency (RF) waves can help solve some challenges in underwater communication. RF waves can propagate longer distances through seawater at very low frequencies (30–300 Hz). However, using low frequencies requires larger antennas and higher transmit power, limiting the feasibility of such systems. Optical wave applications are limited by scattering losses, typically effective for short distances up to 100 meters underwater. Acoustic waves are the primary method for underwater wireless long-range communication, operating at frequencies from 10 Hz to 1 MHz. Short-range underwater wireless communication networks rely on acoustic waves due to their ability to travel long distances underwater. However, acoustic waves reflect off the water surface and cannot transmit information across the water–air boundary effectively.

The application of current underwater communication networks has some limitations. These systems cannot directly communicate across the water–air interface, posing a significant challenge for applications requiring such capabilities. Wireless signals have different wavelengths in water and air, complicating the use of a single signal type for cross-medium communications. Radio waves can travel long distances in the air but lose strength exponentially in water. A digital holographic RF system can provide a reliable solution for detecting acoustic signals at depths of a few meters. The system can detect underwater acoustic waves by capturing scattered and diffracted RF signals. The system can detect and process both acoustic and RF signals, facilitating communication across the water–air boundary. Utilizing digital holography, the system can process data in real-time, enhancing underwater communication.

The integration of digital holographic RF systems into ocean exploration technologies offers a promising solution to the challenges posed by traditional underwater communication methods. By leveraging the capabilities of digital holography to process both RF and acoustic signals, these systems can overcome the limitations of current technologies, enabling reliable communication across the water–air boundary. This advancement is crucial for various applications, including environmental monitoring, resource exploration, and military operations, contributing to a deeper understanding and better management of our oceans.

Digital holographic RF system, which can provide reliable detection of acoustic signals on depths up to a few meters presented in Figure 7.1. Long wavelength RF signal transmission and reception for underwater communication provides some advantages of airborne and sea surface platforms:

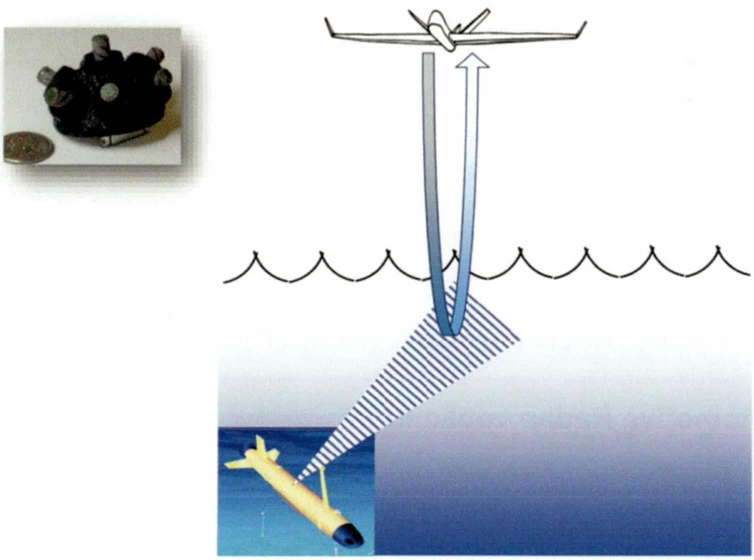

Figure 7.1 Cross-medium wireless system for communication across medium boundaries, specifically across the water–air interface for receiving acoustic signals transmitted from underwater sensors/nodes by radio frequency (RF) transceiver positioned on manned or unmanned airborne or sea surface platforms.

1. Airborne transceiver system with a wide observation area capable of covering a wide observation area to receive acoustic signals transmitted from underwater sensors or nodes. Selection of an optimal frequency range enhances signal penetration and reception. Utilized to suppress surface wave reflections and improve signal detection accuracy.
2. System capable of detecting acoustic signals up to a few meters deep under the sea surface. The system can transmit acoustic signals from depths up to 100 meters toward the sea surface.
3. Airborne platform positioned 1–200 meters above the water surface to transmit and receive electromagnetic signals. System is robust enough to operate in challenging conditions such as sea waves, water splashes, rain, and snow.
4. Wireless communication system can receive acoustic signals transmitted from underwater sensors/nodes without requiring surface devices (US patent pending).

Airborne transceiver system is equipped with an antenna array designed to cover a broad observation area for effective signal reception. It utilizes an optimal frequency range and reference antennas to minimize interference from surface reflections and accurately detect underwater acoustic signals.

The implementation of long-wavelength RF signal transmission and reception from airborne or sea surface platforms presents significant advancements for underwater communication. By leveraging specially designed antenna arrays and optimal frequency ranges, these systems can effectively detect and receive acoustic signals transmitted from underwater sensors or nodes. The robustness of these systems allows them to operate in harsh weather conditions, ensuring reliable communication across the water–air interface. This innovative approach enhances the ability to monitor and explore underwater environments, offering valuable applications in environmental monitoring, resource exploration, and scientific research [1, 2].

7.2 Automotive Radar Application

The integration of next-generation AI-assisted radar systems presents a significant opportunity to enhance autonomous driving capabilities. While LiDAR and camera technologies offer excellent imaging resolution, their effectiveness is often limited in adverse environmental conditions. Imaging and recognition radar technology, on the other hand, has the potential to overcome these limitations, providing robust and reliable performance in various weather conditions.

Application of AI-assisted radar systems provides the following advances:

1. Radar systems maintain consistent performance regardless of rain, snow, or fog, making them ideal for autonomous driving in diverse weather conditions. Radar can work alongside LiDAR and optical camera systems, enhancing overall system reliability and safety, particularly in adverse weather.
2. Radar systems are relatively inexpensive and more affordable compared to LiDAR and can be scaled in advanced driver-assistance systems (ADAS) for widespread use in autonomous vehicles.
3. Unlike cameras and LiDAR, radar systems measure velocity directly, providing crucial data for real-time safety decisions. Distributed RF frequency around vehicle antennas covers a wide observation area, enabling comprehensive situational awareness.

Proposed in Chapters 2, 3, holographic radar technology enables virtual (digital) scanning of the entire observation area, offering extensive possibilities for digital signal processing. Multi-antenna systems provide high-resolution directional accuracy, enabling the rapid detection and recognition of objects. Similar to how cell phones transmit and receive signals through various obstacles, automotive radar can ensure reliable performance even in challenging conditions. Automotive radar systems can operate efficiently, similar to LoRa micro transceivers, which are small, cost-effective, and capable of long-range communication [3–9].

Therefore, the application of AI-assisted radar systems in autonomous driving can significantly enhance the potential of radars, offering robust performance in all weather conditions and providing critical data for safe and reliable vehicle operation. By integrating radar with existing LiDAR and camera systems, autonomous vehicles can achieve a higher level of situational awareness and safety, ensuring dependable performance in diverse driving environments.

Figure 7.2 illustrates the concept of a holographic radar system, which provides virtual scanning of the entire observation area and enables extensive digital signal processing capabilities. This technology, combined with AI, represents a transformative advancement in the field of autonomous driving, promising to elevate safety and reliability to new heights.

Multi-antenna system can provide high-resolution directional accuracy detection and recognition of any object practically instantly. Velocity is the most important for safety provided by automotive systems. Only radar

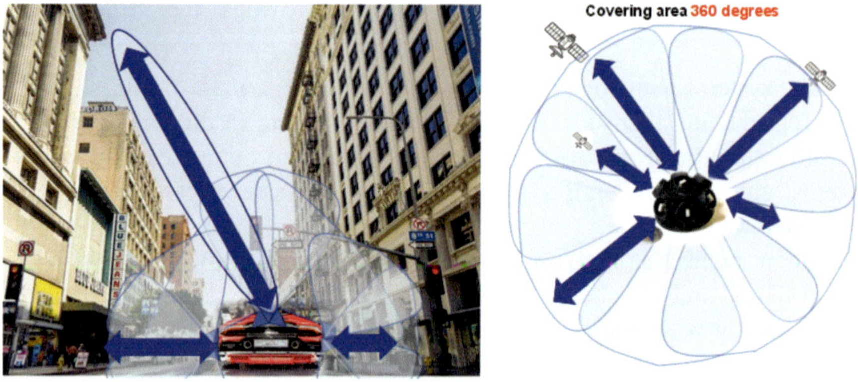

Figure 7.2 Holographic radar provides virtual (digital) scanning of the whole area of observation and wide possibilities for digital signal processing.

measures velocity directly. Camera AI and LiDAR do not measure velocity directly. Radar-based AI systems can fast detect and identify safety conditions by accurately measuring velocity and distance.

7.3 Jamming and Spoofing Protection of Navigation Systems

GPS and other satellite-based navigation systems are particularly susceptible to jamming and spoofing attacks due to their reliance on very low-level signals. These systems can be easily disrupted by inexpensive jammer devices available on the market, as illustrated in Figure 7.3. Vulnerabilities of navigation systems include jamming, the use of low-power devices that emit pseudo-GPS satellite signals, confusing the receiver's correlators, and preventing the receiver from determining a correct position, and spoofing, the creation of counterfeit GPS signals that mislead the receiver into calculating incorrect position, velocity, or timing information.

An effective preliminary defense against jamming involves using an array of directional antennas to spatially filter the direction of incoming navigation signals. This method relies on detecting signals that exceed a pre-established threshold level, as depicted in Figure 7.4.

The directional antenna arrays, which cover the entire sky with relatively narrow observation sections, can significantly enhance protection against jammers. These arrays can switch off receiving channels that do not have satellite signals available for navigation, ensuring enough satellites remain

Figure 7.3 Available on market jammers of navigation systems.

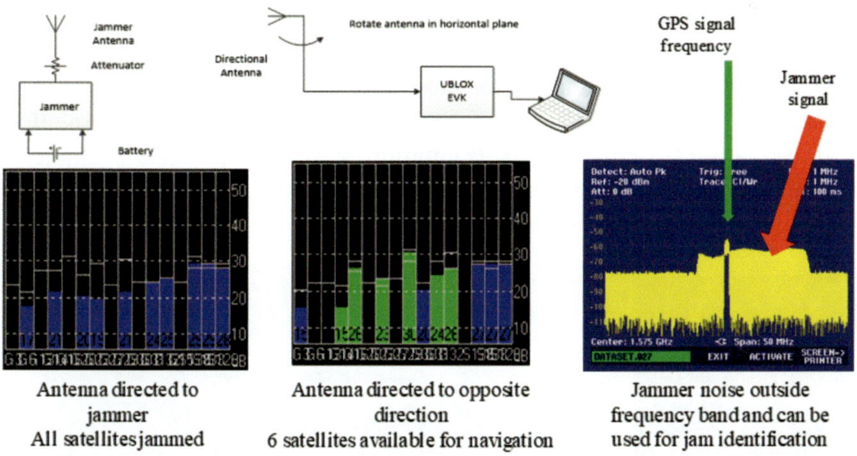

Figure 7.4 Detection of jammed and satellite available for navigation signals by steering direction of GPS antenna. The spectrum of jammer and GPS signals have been applied for the test.

available for accurate positioning. Narrow beamwidth antennas improve the ability to filter out jamming signals based on their direction. If no valid satellite signals are detected in a channel, that channel can be switched off to avoid interference. It ensures that enough satellite signals are available even when some are jammed.

Vehicle bodies can serve as physical barriers against jamming signals. Installing directional antennas around the perimeter of the vehicle provides enhanced protection by utilizing the vehicle body as a shield. This setup is demonstrated in Figure 7.5, where a jammer on a tripod is positioned on one side of the vehicle, and directional antennas are installed on four sides.

GPS vulnerabilities are typically referred to as "jamming" and "spoofing." However, attacking a GPS receiver is not done with the common method of throwing more RF power at the device. A GPS jammer is really a rather low-power device that emits a pseudo GPS satellite signal which confuses the receiver's correlators and prohibits receivers from completing a position solution. The array of directional antennas can provide some preliminary level for the protection of navigation systems by spatial filtering direction of receiving navigation signals if the received signal exceeds the preliminary installed threshold level (Figure 7.4).

The directional antenna array can be efficient for enhancing jammer protection if the antenna array covers the entire sky and directional antennas cover relatively narrow sections of observation. Receiving channels of the navigation system can be switched off if satellite signals in these channels are not available for navigation. The wide covering area of the antenna array will still provide enough satellites for navigation. Jammers need to transmit jamming signals from all directions around the navigation system to jam all or most navigation system channels. If jamming signals are powerful, vehicle bodies can also be used for better protection navigation systems. In this case,

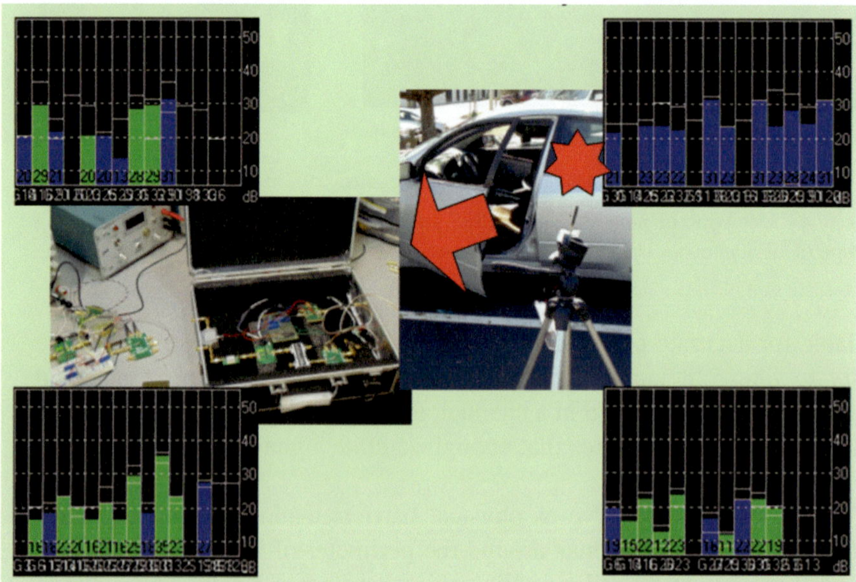

Figure 7.5 Test of a navigation protection system against jammer signal by positioning the receiving array of directional antennas around the perimeter of the ground vehicle.

directional antennas of the navigation system must be installed around the vehicle perimeter. A tripod with the jammer installed on one side of the vehicle and directional antennas of the navigation system are installed on four sides of the vehicle. Jammed and available for navigation signals detected and shown in four directions. The metal vehicle body can provide additional jam protection for the navigation system even if the jammer is positioned relatively close, as shown in Figure 7.5.

Distributed inside a small UAV navigation system with separate shielded directional antennas was tested for protection against jammer signals. Directional antennas with jam protection circuits reacting to signals exceeding threshold level are positioned on four sides of the UAV, and connected with the main processor by digital interfaces as shown in Figure 7.6 [10].

Receiving antenna modules (RAMs) with directional antenna arrays, each coupled with direct detection and digitizing channel can also be distributed around the perimeter of the carrier vehicle. Monopulse processing of signals in distributed antenna arrays provides instant information about received signal sources spectrum signatures and position and filters out jammer of

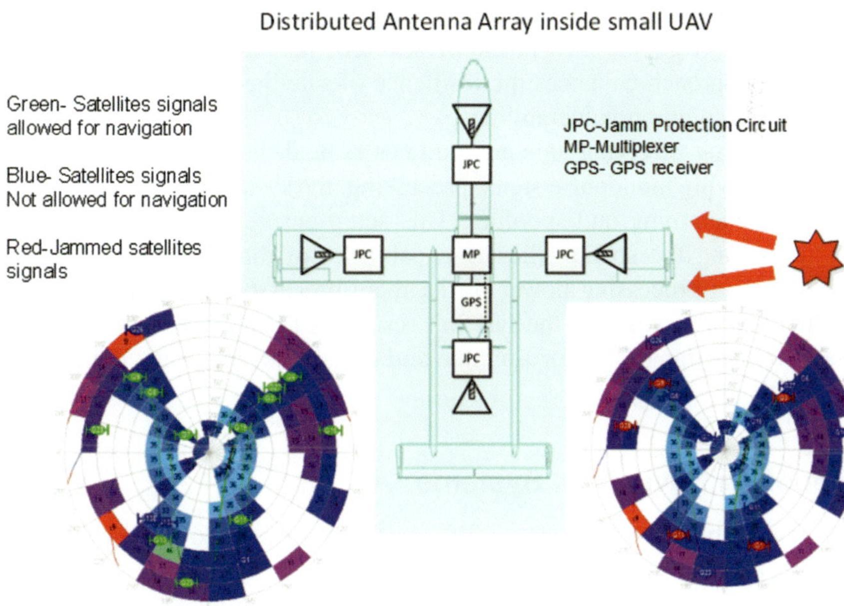

Figure 7.6 Test of a navigation protection system against jammer signal by positioning the receiving array of directional antennas inside a small UAV.

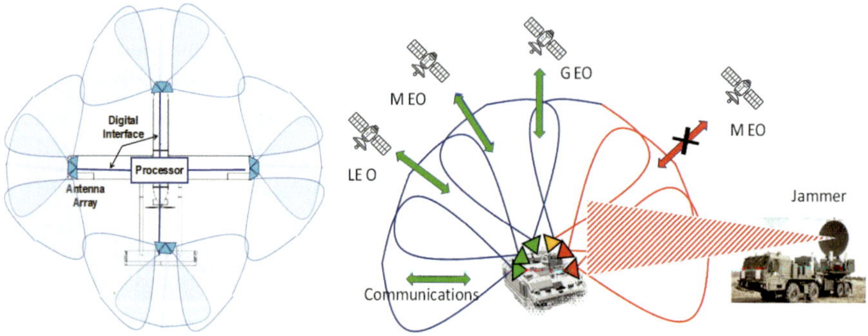

Figure 7.7 Fly eye distributed antenna arrays for navigation, communication, or target detection can provide additional system protection against powerful jammer signals.

spoofing signals by selection by spectrum or spatial position, like shown in Figure 7.7.

The implementation of directional antenna arrays and strategic placement of antennas around vehicle perimeters offers robust protection against jamming and spoofing attacks on navigation systems. By integrating spatial filtering, channel switching, and physical shielding, these methods can ensure reliable navigation even in the presence of jamming attempts. This multi-faceted approach enhances the resilience of satellite-based navigation systems against common vulnerabilities.

By distributing receiving antenna modules around the perimeter of the UAV and employing monopulse signal processing, the system can effectively protect against jamming and spoofing. This setup ensures reliable navigation by leveraging the spatial filtering capabilities of directional antennas and the real-time processing power of the main processor. The distributed architecture not only enhances the system's resilience to interference but also provides a robust framework for accurate and secure navigation in complex environments.

7.4 Spoofing Navigation Systems

Satellite navigation systems, such as GPS, operate based on two fundamental mathematical concepts:

1. Trilateration: positioning derived from three distances.
2. Distance–rate–time relationship: calculation of position based on the distance traveled, speed of travel, and time spent traveling.

7.4.1 Spoofing techniques

Navigation spoofers exploit these principles by re-broadcasting spatial sector signals after a deliberate time delay. Even encrypted timing signals are susceptible to this attack, as spoofing systems do not need to decrypt the received signals; they simply receive, delay, and re-transmit them. This method is extremely effective, requiring relatively low power and being cost-efficient. The GPS receiver correlates the spoofed signals and incorporates the erroneous data into its position solution, as depicted in Figure 7.8.

Spoofing tactics can significantly impact the accuracy of satellite navigation systems by introducing errors into the trilateration process. This can be particularly problematic for applications that rely on precise positioning, such as satellite-guided smart bombs designed for high-precision strikes in all weather conditions.

One effective mitigation strategy involves the use of directional antennas to control the delay of navigation satellite signals in specific spatial direction sectors. Controlling the delay of navigation satellite signals using directional antennas can provide control to the trilateration system which calculates positions by generating signals that exhibit suspicious delays.

An antenna array with directional antennas covering separate areas of observation sectors was applied for test spoofing GPS. Delay of navigation signals allows for dramatic change in the calculated azimuth direction as presented in Figure 7.9.

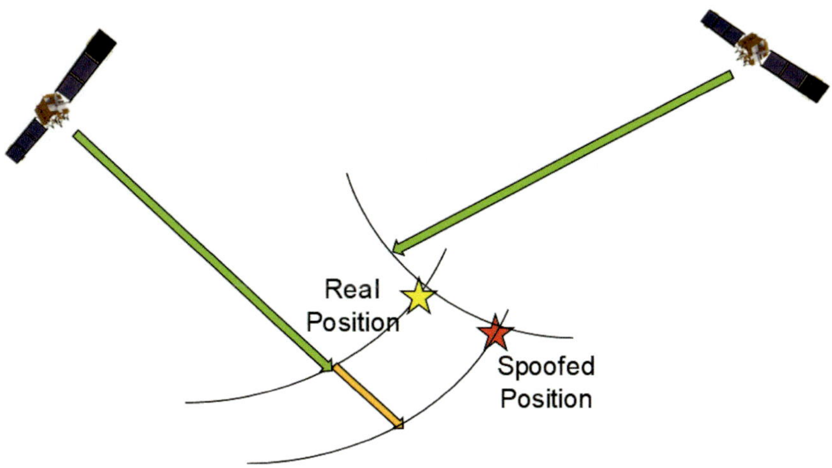

Figure 7.8 Illustration of navigation system spoofing where the receiver incorporates erroneous data due to spoofed signals.

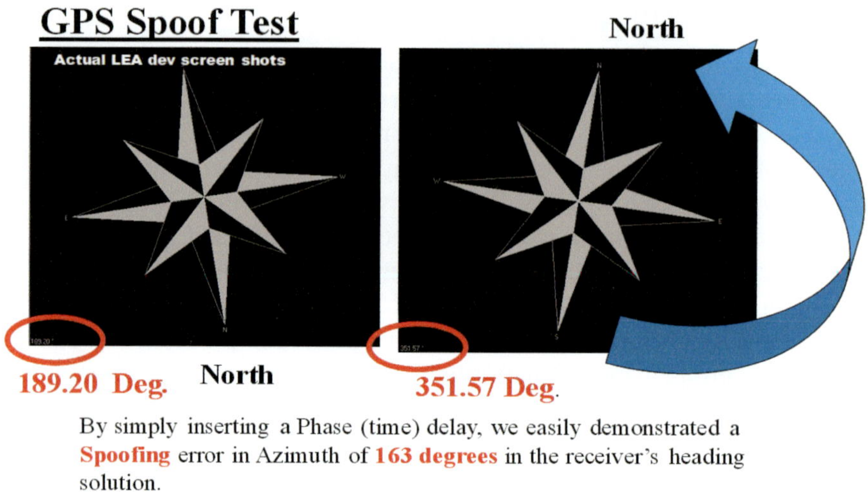

Figure 7.9 Test of the spoofing navigation system. Delay of satellite signals with a controllable directional antenna array allows for change calculated by trilateration azimuth in the navigation system.

The application of directional antennas to control signal delays and detect spoofed signals is a promising approach to safeguarding satellite navigation systems from spoofing attacks. This technique enhances the reliability and accuracy of navigation solutions, particularly in critical applications where precision is paramount. By integrating these mitigation strategies, satellite navigation systems can be made more resilient against sophisticated spoofing tactics.

7.5 Active Distributed Radar Concepts

Active radar systems, which include a transmitter of RF or microwave signals, are highly effective for detecting ground targets and low-altitude targets, particularly when positioned on blimps or towers. These systems are advantageous for various civil applications but are notably vulnerable in battlefield scenarios (Figure 7.10).

Ground-based radar systems face significant challenges in detecting low-altitude drones due to blind zones created by buildings, trees, and other ground-based obstacles. Simply increasing the radar transmitting power does not necessarily enhance the detection range for low-altitude drones, as shown in Figure 7.11.

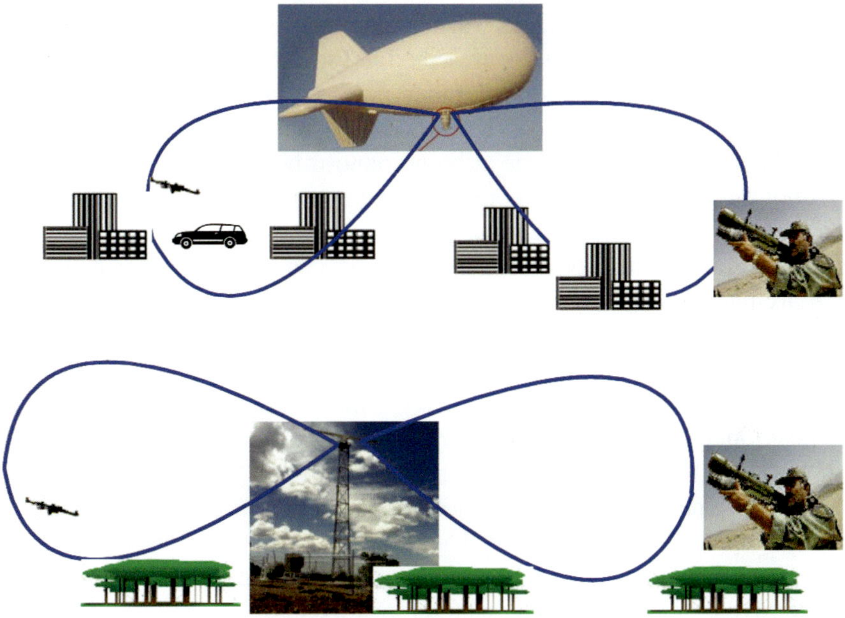

Figure 7.10 Active radar systems positioned on blimps or towers are effective for detection of moving on-ground or low-altitude targets.

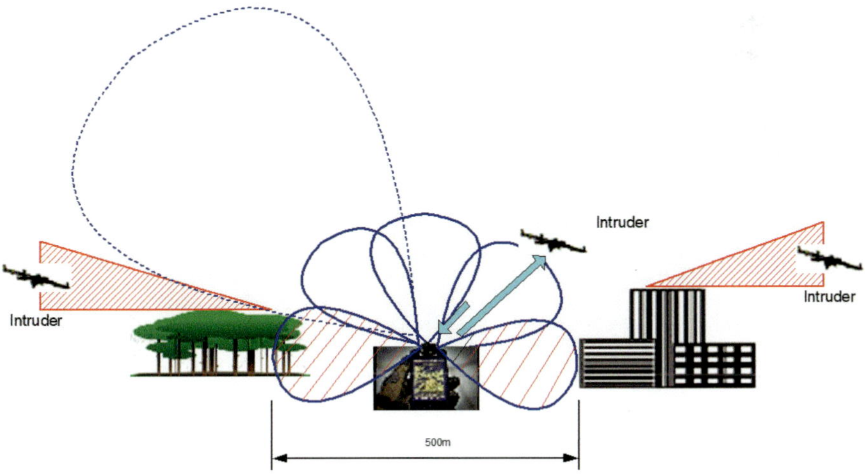

Figure 7.11 Detection of low-altitude moving targets by ground-based active radar system.

To overcome these challenges, a semi-active distributed radar network concept is proposed. This concept involves deploying an active micro-radar network that can consist of stationary distributed units or controllable moving ground or airborne nano-robots, as presented in Figure 7.12.

Invisible semi-active distributed radar network concept based on the application of active micro-radar network based on stationary distributed or controllable moving ground or airborne nano-robots. "Invisible," means passive, not transmitted wireless connected operator receiver receiving information about targets from active radar network (Figures 7.12, 7.13).

High-resolution small power radar systems can be preliminarily distributed around high-sniper risk places. Radar does not need a large range and can have small not easily detectable transmitting power. Passive radar systems can be applied in urban area, where broadcasting signals can be applied. The invisible operator with receiving only passive mapping display can be positioned in wide area around and do not trackable.

An essential feature of this concept is the use of "invisible" passive receivers. These passive receivers do not transmit signals themselves but are wirelessly connected to an operator. They receive information about targets from the active radar network, thus remaining undetected while providing comprehensive coverage and data on target locations.

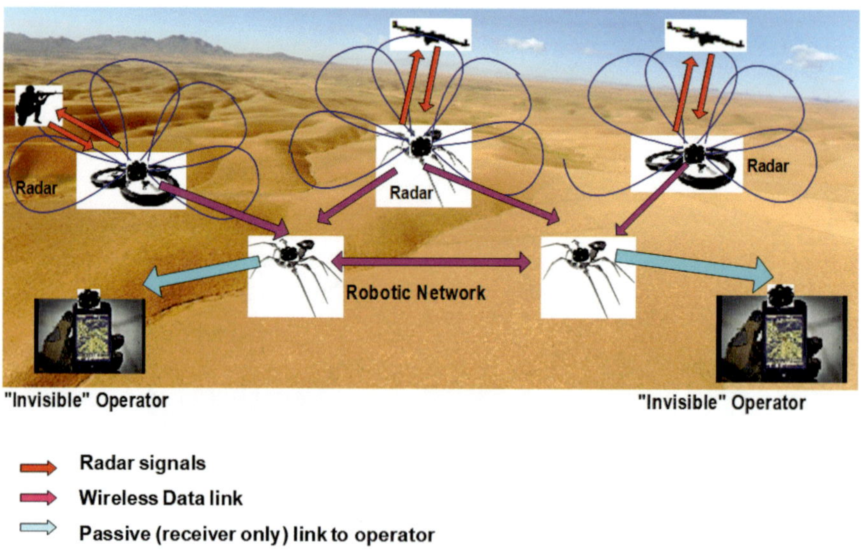

Figure 7.12 Semi-active distributed radar network concept.

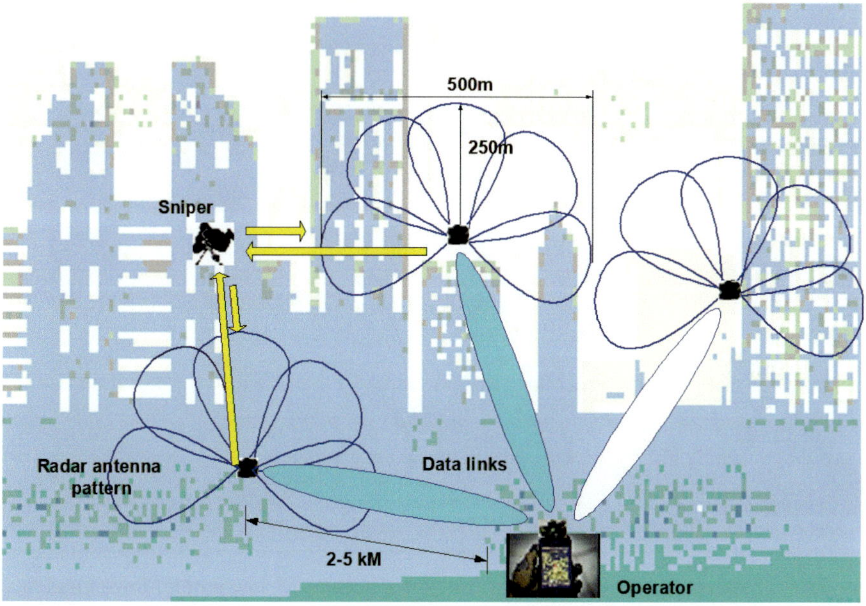

Figure 7.13 Application of semi-active distributed radar network for pre-shot sniper gun detection.

7.6 Passive Distributed Radar Concept

The passive distributed radar network concept leverages non-cooperative satellite and broadcast signals for the detection of low-profile, low-altitude targets. This approach involves the deployment of passive digital holographic radar antenna modules on cell towers distributed along a border or around protected objects. These modules can detect and recognize multiple low-profile targets almost instantly and transfer the information wirelessly or via cables to a central operator [11–13].

The network uses existing satellite and broadcast signals, eliminating the need for dedicated transmitters and reducing the system's detectability. Employing digital holographic radar allows for high-resolution detection and recognition of targets, making it suitable for identifying small, low-profile objects. The system provides nearly instantaneous detection and recognition of targets, with data transmitted to the operator via a digital interface, either wirelessly or through cables.

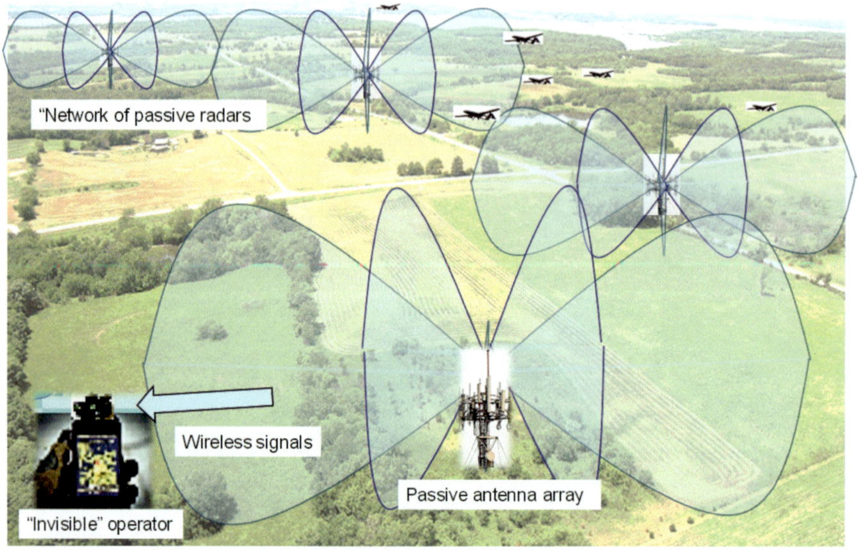

Figure 7.14 Passive distributed radar network for detection of low-profile, low-altitude targets.

By positioning radar modules on cell towers, the network can cover extensive areas, such as borders or zones around protected objects, ensuring comprehensive surveillance. The passive nature of the radar modules and the operator's device enhances the system's stealth, making it less likely to be detected or disrupted by adversaries. The operator can use a portable passive receiver device, which does not transmit signals, allowing for flexible and secure operation within the covered area.

Passive radar modules on cell towers continuously receive and process satellite and broadcast signals. When these signals encounter low-profile, low-altitude targets, they are scattered and diffracted, creating a detectable pattern. The radar modules use digital holographic techniques to analyze the scattered signals, generating high-resolution data on the detected targets. The processed data is transmitted to the operator via a digital interface, providing real-time updates on target locations and characteristics. The operator, equipped with a portable passive receiver device, can monitor the detected targets and receive alerts as necessary. The device can also display detailed information about each target, including its position and movement.

The passive distributed radar network can be deployed along national borders to detect and track unauthorized crossings by low-profile targets, such as drones or small vehicles. By surrounding critical infrastructure with radar modules, the system can provide continuous monitoring and rapid response capabilities to potential threats. The network can also be used for environmental monitoring, detecting wildlife movements, and other natural phenomena in remote or protected areas.

The passive distributed radar network represents a significant advancement in surveillance technology. By utilizing non-cooperative signals and digital holographic radar techniques, this system offers high-resolution detection and recognition capabilities for low-profile, low-altitude targets. Its passive nature enhances stealth and security, making it a valuable tool for border surveillance, critical infrastructure protection, and other applications requiring discreet and reliable monitoring.

Conclusion

The proposed in Chapter 2 technique for object recognition in high-scattering mediums revolves around incorporating the angular spectrum of diffracted/scattered components for Fresnel (near-field) recording of digital object distribution patterns. Key aspects of the proposed technique include:

Overcoming pixel size limitations. The inherent limitations of detection resolution, often constrained by the minimum pixel size, can be transcended by transferring holographic data from time to the frequency domain, where the best resolution is determined by the minimum digital sampling and/or phase measurement step and will be invariant to relatively long radio and microwave wavelengths.

Fourier transform and filtering of the distribution of diffracting components from reference antennas, the technique enables the separation of objects from the surrounding medium based on their spectrum signatures. This approach captures diffraction components containing vital information about an object's dielectric properties, size, and shape, all of which remain unaffected by its spatial position.

Additional information about the object is gleaned by processing the digital hologram signals across the frequency, time, and spatial domains. The spatial domain represents the object's position in space measured by the directions of signal arrival, which are then transformed into phase/time delay. The strategic placement of receiving antennas along multiple axes imparts additional multi-axis information about the object.

The use of long-wavelength radio frequency signals, known for their excellent penetration capabilities, is highlighted. This choice allows for high-resolution imaging and recognition, especially in scenarios with high-scattering conditions.

The implementation of monopulse multi-channel signal processing is emphasized for its role in significantly reducing computational complexity. The application of simple one-step algorithms for object recognition and decision-making is presented as an advantage.

The mention of information remaining invariant to the object's spatial position when radio and microwave wavelengths are long relative to the object's size is crucial. This suggests robustness in recognizing objects regardless of their location.

References

[1] P. A. Molchanov " Seeing Invisible: Advanced Antenna Arrays," River Publishers, Publication date: 04/12/2024, [Online] Available https://www.barnesandnoble.com/w/seeing-invisible-pavlo-a-molchanov/1144371618 [Accessed April 12, 2024].

[2] A. Gorwara, P. Molchanov "Fly Eye Radar Concept," The 18th International Radar Symposium IRS 2017, Prague, Czech Republic, June 28-30, 2017.

[3] P. Molchanov, "Objects Recognition in High-scattering Conditions at Radio/Microwave Frequency," SPIE Defense + Commercial Sensing conference, National Harbor, Washington DC, April, 2024.

[4] P. Molchanov, "Multi-Antenna Array for All Space Communications," 2024 IEEE Radio Wireless Week (RWW) Conference, January, 2024.

[5] P. Molchanov "Tactical radar system for detection of hypersonic missiles and UAS," US patent appl. 17/651,800 02/02/2022.

[6] P. A. Molchanov "Fly Eye Imaging Radar," US patent appl.18100829, 01/24/23.

[7] P. Molchanov "Monopulse synthetic aperture radar," US patent appl. 17/699,129 03/20/2022.

[8] P. Molchanov "Radar for detection of concealed objects," US patent appl. 18/100,882, 01/24/2023.

[9] P. Molchanov "Enhanced RF Medical Imaging System," US patent appl. 18/144,027 05/05/2023.

[10] P. Molchanov, V. Contarino, "Multi-beam Antenna Array for Protecting GPS Receivers from Jamming and Spoofing Signals," [Online] Available http://www.google.com/patents/US20140035783 [Accessed April 12, 2023].

[11] P. Molchanov, "Passive radar system for detection of low-profile low altitude targets," US patent pending, US 2024/0134027 A1, Apr. 25, 2024.
[12] F. Ding, A. Palffy, M. Dariu Gavrila, C. Xiaoxuan Lu, "Hidden Gems: 4D Radar Scene Flow Learning Using Cross-Modal Supervision," IEEE Conference Publication, IEEE Xplore, 2023.
[13] S. E. Lipsky, "Microwave Passive Direction Finder", SciTech Publishing Inc. Raleigh, NC 27613, 2004.

Index

About the Author

Dr. Pavlo A. Molchanov (Senior Member, IEEE) is a highly accomplished professional with an impressive educational background and extensive experience in the field of radar and antenna engineering. He received his M.Sc. degree from the Radio Technical and Electronic Devices Department of Kyiv Polytechnical Institute, Ukraine. He later obtained his Ph.D. degree from the Radio Electronics Department of Moscow Aviation Institute (MAI) in Moscow, USSR, in 1971 and 1980, respectively. He has been a US citizen from 2003. Dr. Molchanov has made significant contributions to the field of design of antenna arrays for low altitude missiles. He has been a Principal Investigator in various projects funded by the US Air Force Small Business Innovation Research (AF SBIR) program and the Office of Naval Research (ONR). In these roles, he designed LIDAR/RADAR systems, protected GPS systems, and developed sense and avoid antenna arrays for US Navy Ships and Naval Aviation.

Dr. Molchanov's expertise is well-documented through his extensive publication record, which includes 250 publications, 5 textbooks, and 20 patents. His work has significantly contributed to the advancement of engineering and technology in the field of advanced antenna arrays and related areas.

For Product Safety Concerns and Information please contact our
EU representative GPSR@taylorandfrancis.com Taylor & Francis
Verlag GmbH, Kaufingerstraße 24, 80331 München, Germany